Constitutional Law in New Zealand

Constitutional Law in New Zealand

Second Edition

Anthony H. Angelo

This book was originally published as a monograph in the International Encyclopaedia of Laws/Constitutional Law.

General Editors: Roger Blanpain, Frank Hendrickx
Volume Editors: André Alen, David Haljan

Wolters Kluwer

Published by:
Kluwer Law International
PO Box 316
2400 AH Alphen aan den Rijn
The Netherlands
Website: www.wklawbusiness.com

Sold and distributed in North, Central and South America by:
Aspen Publishers, Inc.
7201 McKinney Circle
Frederick, MD 21704
United States of America
Email: customer.service@aspenpublishers.com

Sold and distributed in all other countries by:
Turpin Distribution Services Ltd.
Stratton Business Park
Pegasus Drive, Biggleswade
Bedfordshire SG18 8TQ
United Kingdom
Email: kluwerlaw@turpin-distribution.com

ISBN 978-90-411-6641-8

This title is available on www.kluwerlawonline.com

The Author

A.H. Angelo is Professor of Law at the Victoria University of Wellington, where he was Dean of the Faculty of Law from 1991 to 1994. His training and interests are in the fields of foreign and comparative law and constitutional law, and he has had a long involvement with constitutional and legal reform developments in a number of small States in the world.

In the South Pacific, he has had a number of constitutional roles which have related, at various times, to Norfolk Island, Solomon Islands, Niue, Tokelau and the Cook Islands. He is currently Constitutional Advisor to Niue, and Legal Advisor to the Government of Tokelau. Additionally, he was a member of the working party that established the Law School at the University of the South Pacific, and was for a number of years Visiting Professor to the Université Française du Pacifique (Papeete campus).

Publications of constitutional significance include the primary collections – *Laws of Mauritius*, *Mauritius Law Reports*, the Norfolk Island Reprint collection, the *Niue Laws*, the *Laws of Tokelau*, *Cook Islands Laws* – and *Leading Cases of Seychelles* 1988–2010.

Seminal contributions to legal literature have appeared in a number of periodicals particularly in relation to the legal systems of Tokelau, Mauritius and Seychelles.

Professor Angelo is an Academicien of the International Academy of Comparative Law and President of the New Zealand Association for Comparative Law.

The Author

Table of Contents

Table of Contents

List of Abbreviations

ANZCERTA	Australia-New Zealand Closer Economic Relations Trade Agreement
CERD	Committee on the Elimination of Racial Discrimination
FPP	First-Past-the-Post
GST	Goods and Services Tax
IDEA	Institute for Democracy and Electoral Assistance
MMP	Mixed Member Proportional
PV	Preferential Voting
SM	Supplementary Member System
STV	Single Transferable Vote
USP	University of the South Pacific

List of Abbreviations

General Introduction

§1. CONSTITUTIONAL HISTORY[1]

1. The human habitation of New Zealand probably began in the eighth century AD,[2] when migrants arrived from Eastern Polynesia. The society these migrants brought was organized and defined, but there was nothing which would be understood as constitutional government in modern Western terms. Society was based on tribal, sub-tribal and extended family groupings which were largely autonomous.

2. Despite European discovery of New Zealand in 1642 by the Dutch explorer Abel Janszoon Tasman, frequent contact with outsiders did not begin until 1769 when the British navigator James Cook arrived. Cook claimed New Zealand for the United Kingdom, but this claim was not formalized.[3]

The British government appointed Justices of the Peace in 1814 and 1819 to exercise some degree of control over British subjects, but otherwise kept its distance from New Zealand affairs, as evidenced by an 1817 Act which officially disavowed any claim over New Zealand's sovereignty.[4]

Indeed there was little contact between New Zealand and the United Kingdom until 1832. At that time the non-Polynesian population was comprised of predominantly sealers, whalers and traders, escaped convicts from Australia and missionaries.

Between 1823 and 1828 the jurisdiction of the courts of New South Wales was extended to British subjects in New Zealand.

3. Eventually a large population of British residents, French colonial aspirations and increased lawlessness provoked action by the British Government. A British Resident was appointed in 1832 and in 1839 the British Government decided to acquire sovereignty over New Zealand. Letters Patent were issued to extend the

1. Information on New Zealand's constitutional history may be found in J.L. Robson, *New Zealand: The Development of Its Laws and Constitution* (2d ed., Stevens and Sons 1967), and P.A. Joseph, *Constitutional and Administrative Law in New Zealand* (4th ed., Brookers 2014).
2. K. Sinclair, *A History of New Zealand* 14 (rev. ed., Penguin 2000).
3. Maori refer to New Zealand as Aotearoa (translates as 'the land of the long white cloud'). For a discussion on early contact between Maori and Europeans, *see,* A. Salmond, *Two Worlds: First Meetings between Maori and Europeans 1642–1772* (Viking 1991).
4. 57 Geo 3, Ch. 53 'An Act for the more effectual Punishment of Murders and Manslaughters committed in Places not within His Majesty's Dominions'.

boundaries of the New South Wales Colony so that New Zealand could be included as part of that Colony.

4. The Treaty of Waitangi, a treaty between Queen Victoria of the United Kingdom and over 500 Maori chiefs, was signed during 1840. The exact status and meaning of the Treaty are still debated today, particularly since there are several copies and textual differences between the Maori and English versions. It was a pact by which Maori ceded sovereignty to the British Crown, in exchange for the rights and privileges of British subjects, whilst retaining 'the full exclusive and undisturbed possession of their Lands and Estates Forests Fisheries and other properties'.[5]

5. British sovereignty was proclaimed in 1840[6] and New Zealand became a separate Colony from 1841 with its own Executive and Legislative Councils. In 1841, the Consul, Captain William Hobson, was appointed Governor of New Zealand responsible to the Queen via the Colonial Office in London. The Governor was advised by a small Executive Council comprising the Colonial Secretary, the Attorney-General and the Colonial Treasurer, and presided over the Legislative Council which comprised the Governor, the Colonial Secretary, the Attorney-General, the Colonial Treasurer and three Justices of the Peace. In 1846, by statute, Her Majesty divided the islands into Provinces which had their own legislatures and also provided for a general legislature with specified law-making powers.[7] From 1852 the New Zealand Constitution Act (UK)[8] of the British Parliament provided for the establishment of provincial government as well as a colonial General Assembly. The General Assembly consisted of the Governor, an appointed Legislative Council and an elected House of Representatives. New Zealand thus became a self-governing colony, with 'responsible government'. The New Zealand Parliament was empowered to pass laws for 'the peace, order, and good government of New Zealand'.[9] The New Zealand Parliament could not, however, enact a law which conflicted with the law of England or which had extra-territorial effect. Gradually, the

5. Literature on the Treaty is extensive. Some notable contributions are C. Orange, *The Treaty of Waitangi* (Allen and Unwin (NZ) Ltd 1989); I. Kawharu (ed.), *Waitangi: Maori and Pakeha Perspectives on the Treaty of Waitangi* (Oxford U. Press 1989); J. Kelsey, A *Question of Honour?: Labour and the Treaty, 1984–1989* (Allen and Unwin 1990); P. McHugh, *The Maori Magna Carta: New Zealand Law and the Treaty of Waitangi* (Oxford U. Press 1991); W. Renwick, *Sovereignty and Indigenous Rights: The Treaty of Waitangi in International Contexts* (Victoria U. Press 1991); Phil Parkinson, *Preserved in the Archives of the Colony: The English Drafts of the Treaty of Waitangi* (N.Z. Assn. Comp. L. 2005); Richard Boast, *Buying the Land, Selling the Land* (Victoria U. Press 2008); Mathew Palmer, *Treaty of Waitangi in New Zealand's Law and Constitution* (Victoria U. Press 2008).
6. A proclamation was issued on 21 May 1840, proclaiming Her Majesty's sovereignty in the North Island on the basis of cession. A second proclamation gave Her Majesty sovereignty in the South Island on the grounds of discovery. For the creation of the colony of New Zealand, *see,* 3 and 4 Vict, Ch. 62.
7. 9 and 10 Vict, Ch. 103.
8. 15 and 16 Vict, Ch. 72.
9. Section 53.

powers of the New Zealand Parliament were widened. In 1857, the British Parliament conferred on the New Zealand Parliament the power to amend most of the Constitution Act 1852.[10]

In 1865, the Colonial Laws Validity Act (UK) provided that colonial laws were void only if repugnant to Imperial Statutes and Orders extending to the Colonies.[11] This provided further evidence of New Zealand's growing independent status. Government became increasingly centralized and the Provincial Council System was abolished in 1876.[12] In 1907, in recognition of its developing independence, New Zealand attained Dominion status.

6. Two World Wars saw New Zealand exercising more individuality in foreign affairs, despite official Imperial control of these matters. The Imperial Conference on the Operation of Dominion Legislation 1929 sought ways to make the legal position match the realities of the relations between Great Britain and its colonies. This led to the Statute of Westminster 1931 (UK).[13] New Zealand's Parliament adopted that Act in 1947,[14] and thereby removed the doctrine of repugnancy and the inability to enact extra-territorial legislation, and achieved full independence. At the same time the United Kingdom Parliament undertook not to enact legislation for New Zealand without New Zealand's explicit request and consent and New Zealand obtained United Kingdom authority to amend all of the 1852 Constitution Act.

7. In 1950, the upper house of Parliament, the Legislative Council, was abolished.[15] Since then, there has been little change to the outward forms of the Constitution. Many of New Zealand's constitutional rules were (and still are) found in constitutional convention. As a result of problems in relation to the transfer of power after the 1984 General Election, some of the basic constitutional rules were set in statutory form, and the Constitution Act 1852 was repealed by the Constitution Act 1986. The Constitution Act 1986 is an ordinary, unentrenched statute[16] which provides, in skeletal form, for some matters relating to the legislature, the executive, the Head of State and the judiciary.

§2. Profile of the Form of Government

8. New Zealand is a constitutional monarchy. The Queen of New Zealand is the sovereign and the Head of State.[17] The royal powers of the monarch may be

10. New Zealand Constitution Amendment Act 1857 (UK), 20 and 21 Vict, Ch. 53.
11. 28 and 29 Vict, Ch. 63.
12. Abolition of the Provinces Act 1875.
13. 22 Geo 5, Ch. 4.
14. Statute of Westminster Adoption Act 1947, New Zealand Constitution Amendment (Request and Consent) Act 1947. New Zealand Constitution Amendment Act 1947 (UK).
15. Legislative Council Abolition Act 1950.
16. The exception is s. 17 relating to the term of Parliament.
17. Constitution Act 1986, s. 2.

exercised by the Governor-General of New Zealand by delegation under the Letters Patent of 1983.[18]

9. Parliament holds the power in New Zealand government. However, the party or parties which control a majority in the House of Representatives dominate the executive through Cabinet and have the power to ensure that legislation implementing party policy passes through Parliament and becomes law.

In practice, the responsibilities of an executive government are performed by the Ministers of the Crown. Ministers are members of Parliament and are drawn, by constitutional convention, from among members of the party which holds the majority of seats in Parliament.[19] The Ministers form the Cabinet[20] which is headed by the party leader, the Prime Minister. The Prime Minister is an ordinary Member of Parliament with no extra statutory powers. Cabinet formulates Government policy, and individual Ministers control Government departments to ensure the effective implementation of Government policy.

10. Parliament consists of the Sovereign in right of New Zealand and the House of Representatives.[21] By convention, the Governor-General's or Sovereign's function is almost purely formal and performed on the advice of the responsible Minister. Bills require the assenting signature of the Governor-General in order to become law.[22] Parliament has full power to make laws, and it controls all the spending of public money.[23]

Elections to Parliament are conducted under the Electoral Act 1993. This Act contains some partially entrenched provisions. They relate to the term of Parliament, the Representation Commission, the method of determining electoral boundaries, the quota, the voting age and the method of voting.[24] In 1995, the House of Representatives had ninety-nine members but at the next election the number increased to 120 members with the change to the electoral system of Mixed Member Proportional (MMP) Representation. The term of a Parliament is three years.[25] The Governor-General is responsible for the prorogation, dissolution and summoning of the New Zealand Parliament.[26]

11. The judiciary in New Zealand is separate from the politics of Parliament and the Cabinet influence on the executive, although the members of the judiciary are

18. Letters Patent Constituting the Office of the Governor-General of New Zealand, SR 1983/225, as amended by SR 1987/8 and SR 2006/224.
19. Following the change in 1996 of the electoral system, discussed below, there are now also commonly Ministers and Associate Ministers appointed from minority parties which form part of the Government as a result of confidence and supply agreements with the party holding the majority of seats in Parliament.
20. There may also be Ministers outside Cabinet.
21. Constitution Act 1986, s. 14.
22. Section 16.
23. Section 22.
24. Electoral Act 1993, *see,* ss 28, 35, 36, 74 and 168 and s. 17(1) of the Constitution Act 1986. *See,* s. 268 of the Electoral Act 1993.
25. Constitution Act s. 17(1).
26. Section 18.

appointed by the executive. The highest New Zealand Court is the Supreme Court.[27] It is composed of a Chief Justice and four or five judges, appointed by the Governor-General on the advice of the Attorney-General. The Chief Justice presides. The Court of Appeal, established under the Judicature Act 1908, hears appeals from the High Court and District Courts. The High Court, also established under the Judicature Act 1908, is a superior court of general jurisdiction.[28] The District Courts are the principal inferior courts; they are governed by the District Courts Act 1947.

The Constitution Act 1986 protects the tenure of High Court Judges (which includes Court of Appeal and Supreme Court Judges) and prevents the reduction of their salaries.[29]

Though the Acts which relate to the judiciary form an important part of the Constitution, they are not protected as special legislation in any way.

§3. TERRITORY

12. The vast majority of New Zealand residents live in the two main islands, the North Island and the South Island. Together these islands comprise about 270,550 km^2; 118,777 km^2 in the North and 151,215 km^2 in the South. New Zealand's territory is defined in the New Zealand Boundaries Act 1863.[30] This territory is within the boundaries drawn from 162 degrees East and 173 degrees West longitude, and 33 degrees and 53 degrees South latitude. These boundaries include Stewart Island and the Chatham Islands and several other remote, sparsely populated islands. The Kermadec Islands Act 1887 enlarged New Zealand's boundaries to include the Kermadec Group.

In addition, New Zealand has exercised jurisdiction over the Ross Dependency in Antarctica since 1923, and Tokelau since 1926.[31] The Ross Dependency comprises the land, islands and ice-shelf of Antarctica between 160 East and 150 West. Tokelau consists of three tropical atolls whose total land area amounts to about 12 km^2.

New Zealand has also been responsible, at various times, for Samoa, the Cook Islands and Niue. These States are no longer part of New Zealand, although the latter two maintain links in the areas of foreign affairs, defence and citizenship as associated States.

New Zealand's main islands are relatively isolated from the rest of the world. Australia is the country's nearest neighbour of substantial size, and that is 1,600 km distant. This isolation has had a significant impact on New Zealand's domestic and international policy.

---

27. Established by the Supreme Court Act 2003.
28. In 2012, the Law Commission published a report entitled *Review of the Judicature Act 1908: Towards a New Courts Act* (NZLC R126, 2012). The Judicature Modernisation Bill is intended to implement the Government's response to that Report, and to replace the Judicature Act 1908. The Bill passed its second reading in February 2015 and is likely to be enacted some time in 2015.
29. Sections 23 and 24.
30. 26 and 27 Vict, Ch. 23. The Preamble and s. 2 of this Act remain in force in New Zealand: *see,* the Imperial Laws Application Act 1988.
31. *See,* Part III, Ch. 2, Component States.

13. In the North and South Islands of New Zealand and in all other islands except the Chatham Islands, Tokelau and the associated States, uniform time is maintained in New Zealand. Approximately between the first Sunday in April and the last Sunday in September New Zealand Standard Time operates. This is twelve hours ahead of Coordinated Universal Time. Between September and April New Zealand Daylight Time operates, bringing New Zealand time thirteen hours ahead of Coordinated Universal Time. The Chatham Islands is forty-five minutes ahead of New Zealand.[32]

§4. State Population: Demography

14. The population at the time of the 2013 Census was 4,242,048, with an annual growth rate of 0.7%. The growth rate stems from natural increase and migration. Figures put New Zealand's natural increase for 2014 at 26,179, that is 57,242 births minus 31,063 deaths. The provisional fertility rate in 2014 showed that the average New Zealand woman would bear 1.9 children during her lifetime. The recent trend in New Zealand migration has been for immigrants to outnumber those emigrating.

15. Life expectancy in New Zealand stands at 79.6 years for males and 83.3 for females.

16. The provisional ratio of males to females in New Zealand in 2014 was 96.1 males for every 100 females.

17. The predominant racial group in New Zealand is of European origin. Approximately 74% of New Zealand's population identified with this ethnic group in 2006, with 15.6% identifying themselves as New Zealand Maori, 12.2% as Asian and 7.8% as of Pacific Island ethnicity.

18. Within New Zealand, approximately 77% (or 3,540,800) of the people live in the North Island.

19. New Zealand's rural population in percentage terms has steadily declined over the past fifty years. Eighty-six per cent of New Zealanders live in urban areas. Fourteen per cent live in rural areas.

32. Time Act 1974.

Part I. Sources of Constitutional Law

Chapter 1. Treaties

20. According to accepted Common Law doctrine, 'any rights purporting to be conferred by … a treaty of cession cannot be enforced in the courts, except insofar as they have been incorporated in the municipal law'.[33] Thus, there exists a sense in which no treaty is a source of New Zealand constitutional law. Rather, the municipal law giving effect to it is the source of the law. The usual form of this incorporation into municipal law is by Act of Parliament.

21. New Zealand is an active member of the international community of nations and as such is party to many treaties and covenants.[34] Thus, for example, the New Zealand Bill of Rights Act 1990 and the Human Rights Act 1993 affirm New Zealand's commitment to the International Covenant on Civil and Political Rights.

New Zealand ratified the International Covenant on Civil and Political Rights in 1978 and accepted the Optional Protocol to the Covenant on Civil and Political Rights in 1989. New Zealand is also a party to other International Covenants such as the International Covenant on Economic, Social and Cultural Rights which it ratified in 1978 and the Convention on the Elimination of all Forms of Discrimination against Women ratified in 1984.

22. The position of the Treaty of Waitangi is somewhat different because of its role and the nature of the parties. In current theory the treaty is usually regarded as a basic constitutional document. Sir Robin Cooke, then President of the Court of Appeal approved the notion that 'the Treaty is a document relating to fundamental rights'.[35] According to this view, the Maori chiefs ceded sovereignty to the Crown, including the rights to make laws, to govern and to dispense justice, in exchange for the protection of their possessions and the right to be British subjects. The Treaty of Waitangi is a source of law in the sense that it gives legitimacy to the Crown government.[36]

---

33. *Hoani Te Heuheu Tukino v. Aotea District Maori Land Board* [1941] AC 308, 324.
34. As of 2012, New Zealand was party to approximately 1500 international treaties: Ministry of Foreign Affairs and Trade *International Treaties List: July 2012*.
35. *New Zealand Maori Council v. Attorney-General* [1987] 1 NZLR 641, 655–656. *See also, Te Runanganui o Te Ika Whenua Inc. Society v. Attorney-General* [1994] 2 NZLR 20.
36. G. Palmer, *Unbridled Power: An Interpretation of New Zealand's Constitution and Government* 19 (2d ed., Oxford U. Press 1987).

23. Another very important treaty is the Australia-New Zealand Closer Economic Relations Trade Agreement (ANZCERTA or CER) which was concluded between Australia and New Zealand in 1983. It is an extensive trade agreement which has resulted, since 1990, in the removal of tariffs and quantitative restrictions on all goods passing between the two countries. It also deals with matters such as industry assistance and quarantine and customs procedures. In recent years, New Zealand has signed a number of other free trade agreements, including agreements with China in 2008, with ASEAN and Malaysia in 2010, and with Hong Kong in 2011.

Chapter 2. Constitution

24. New Zealand's Constitution is the sum of the rules which govern the organization of the affairs of the State and the relationship of the State with individuals. New Zealand has no single document, entrenched or otherwise, that could be called the Constitution. Thus the 'Constitution' can be changed by statute using ordinary procedures. No single document defines the allocation of power between the various areas of Government nor specifies how the various areas are to be organized. Although the Constitution Act 1986 recognizes the existence of the Head of State, the Executive, the Legislature and the Judiciary, it does little more than codify some pre-existing conventions relating to these institutions.

The Constitution Act 1986, for example, provides for the election of the Speaker, states the full powers of the New Zealand Parliament to make law for New Zealand, establishes Parliament's three-year term, provides for the summoning, proroguing and dissolution of Parliament, and protects judges from being removed from office or having their salaries reduced.[37]

These provisions are in no way supreme or entrenched law. The exception is the provision on the Parliamentary term. That is governed by section 268 of the Electoral Act 1993 which requires a 75% majority in the House of Representatives or a majority at a poll of electors in the General and Maori electoral districts before the provision can be amended or repealed. It should be noted, however, that section 268 is not itself entrenched and could be repealed by a simple majority in the House of Representatives.

37. *See,* ss 6, 12, 15, 17, 18, 23 and 24.

Chapter 3. Legislation

25. Many key constitutional provisions are found in the statute book. Many organs of government are defined and their powers limited by statute.

26. Some of the pillars of constitutional law in New Zealand are statutes of British origin. This situation arose because of the English Laws Act 1858, which enacted that the statutes of the United Kingdom as on 14 January 1840, so far as applicable, were New Zealand law. Consequently, a provision of the Magna Carta of 1297[38] and of the Bill of Rights 1688,[39] as well as other key constitutional statutes of the United Kingdom have found their way into New Zealand law. This was recognized in New Zealand by the Imperial Laws Application Act 1988 which specified the relevant laws and declared that they are New Zealand law. The Magna Carta guaranteed individual freedoms; the Bill of Rights 1688 sought to regulate the powers of the Crown and Parliament, and for instance forbade any attempt to suspend law without Parliamentary consent or to raise taxes except with Parliamentary consent.

27. Most New Zealand Acts with constitutional significance relate to the institutions of Government and the limitations on them. Some, however, such as the New Zealand Bill of Rights Act 1990 and the Official Information Act 1982, declare a constitutional principle which affirms rights or imposes certain limitations on official action. The 1990 Act declares New Zealand's commitment to the International Covenant on Civil and Political Rights, and requires that all governmental action be consistent with the rights in the Act.[40]

28. The Official Information Act 1982 regulates Government handling of information; government operates on the presumption that information will be available to the public.[41] In conjunction with the Ombudsmen Act 1975, this provides a useful check on the exercise of public power in New Zealand. So too do the Treaty of Waitangi Act 1975, the Human Rights Act 1993 and the Privacy Act 1993.

29. The electoral process is governed by the Electoral Act 1993. This regulates *inter alia* the qualifications necessary to be elected as a Member of Parliament or to vote in elections, and the procedures for conducting elections.

30. The Supreme Court was constituted by the Supreme Court Act 2003. The High Court and Court of Appeal are constituted under the Judicature Act 1908; the District Courts are governed by the District Courts Act 1947.

38. 25 Edw 1, Ch. 29 is still in force.
39. 1 Will and Mar, Sess 2, Ch. 2. The Title and Preamble, s. 1 (read subject to certain enactments of the New Zealand parliament) and s. 2 are still in force. *See,* the Imperial Laws Application Act 1988, section and First Schedule.
40. Section 3.
41. Section 5.

Chapter 4. Case Law

31. Much of New Zealand's important constitutional common law is found in decisions of English courts handed down hundreds of years ago. The Imperial Laws Application Act 1988 states that the Common Law of England (including the principles of Equity) insofar as it applied to New Zealand before the commencement of the Imperial Laws Application Act 1988 continues in force.[42] Consequently, decisions of constitutional significance of English courts, such as *Prohibitions del Roy*[43] *Case of Proclamations*,[44] the *Case of Ship Money*[45] and *Entick v. Carrington*[46] form part of the fabric of New Zealand's constitutional law. Key New Zealand constitutional decisions have affirmed the distinctions between the various arms of government. The judiciary has pronounced that the Prime Minister as a member of the executive may not act to suspend the law without an Act of Parliament,[47] and that executive action may not contravene the law.[48]

32. The decisions of the New Zealand courts have a further constitutional impact as a result of the judicial review of administrative action. This area of decision-making places a constitutional check on the executive by ensuring that the executive acts reasonably within its powers and fairly. Similarly, subsidiary legislation must be within the powers of the principal Act, or it is void.

33. Because so much of New Zealand's Constitution is found in legislation, judicial interpretation and comment form an important part of the New Zealand constitution. So too do the decisions of judges in other common law jurisdictions.

42. Section 5.
43. (1607) 12 Co Rep 63.
44. (1611) 12 Co Rep 74.
45. (1637) 3 St Tr 826 (also known as *R v. Hampden*).
46. (1765) 19 St Tr 1030. Government power must be granted by Parliament, the highest sovereign authority within a State; the executive may not take the power unto itself.
47. *Fitzgerald v. Muldoon* [1976] 2 NZLR 615.
48. *Transport Ministry v. Payn* [1977] 2 NZLR 50. This case held that in the absence of any direct statutory authority a traffic officer had no right to enter a property forcibly in pursuit of an offender. Legislation was subsequently passed to change this: *see*, s. 119 of the Land Transport Act 1998.

Chapter 5. Customary Law, Unwritten Law, General Principles of Law

34. New Zealand's Constitution is also found in constitutional convention. Wherever an area of constitutional law is not covered by statute or has not been the subject of a judicial pronouncement, there is probably a constitutional convention concerning it.

35. Constitutional conventions are typically unwritten rules defining the relations between those involved in the constitutional framework. They are usually adhered to because those involved see the wisdom behind the custom, and because they do not wish to appear to be acting unconstitutionally.

Establishment of a convention is usually by gradual practice culminating in a binding rule. One writer, however, has observed that practice by itself and indeed precedent by itself is insufficient to establish a convention. In addition, the creation of the convention requires that there be a reason vis-à-vis the political system for the convention:

> We have to ask ourselves three questions: first, what are the precedents; secondly, did the actors in the precedents believe that they were bound by a rule; and thirdly, is there a reason for the rule? A single precedent with a good reason may be enough to establish the rule. A whole string of precedents without such a reason will be of no avail, unless it is perfectly certain that the persons concerned regarded them as bound by it.[49]

In New Zealand, the relations between the executive and the legislature abound with examples of constitutional convention. The Governor-General conventionally acts only on Ministerial advice. The Cabinet and the office of Prime Minister are creatures of convention.

Although conventions affect the operation of law, they are not themselves laws. Courts may choose to recognize them as an aid to interpreting the law, but they are not enforceable in the courts.

36. Further unwritten law exists in the areas of the royal prerogative. The royal prerogative is the residue of the extensive feudal power once enjoyed by the sovereign, which has not been legislated for by Parliament. In practice, in New Zealand, these prerogative powers are vested in the Governor-General. However, the convention of consultation means that most prerogative powers are only used on advice from Ministers. Prerogative powers include the declaration of war, the granting of pardons and the conferment of honours.

37. There is nothing explicit in the constitutional rules about conventions – but they exist in an environment that accepts the principles of democratic government, human rights, the rule of law and the separation of powers.

49. Sir I. Jennings, *The Law and the Constitution* 136 (5th ed., U. London Press Ltd 1959), 136.

Chapter 6. Subordinate Rules and Regulations

38. Though little of New Zealand's Constitution is contained in subordinate legislation, such legislation is an important source of law. The main form of subordinate legislation is government regulations which are made by the Governor-General in Council or by a Minister.

39. Usually, such subsidiary legislation only expands on or regulates what is stipulated in the principal enactment. Thus, the Electoral Regulations 1996 provide for the mechanics of voter registration and for matters such as special votes.

40. Rules are used for specifying procedural formalities – typically rules of courts. For example, the High Court Rules are made pursuant to the Judicature Act 1908. Bylaws are made by local authorities and other bodies having limited geographic extension; many are made pursuant to the Local Government Act 2002. Bylaws have little constitutional significance. The capacity of local government to make bylaws is strictly limited to areas delegated by central government in local government legislation. They are therefore of exclusively local concern.

41. The Standing Orders of the House of Representatives were originally a form of subsidiary legislation made pursuant to the New Zealand Constitution Act 1852 (UK) and subject to the Governor-General's approval. The House of Representatives now has sole control over its Standing Orders.

Chapter 7. Codification, Interpretation and Hierarchy of Legal Rules

§1. Codification and Interpretation

42. The casuistic nature of the New Zealand legal system is antagonistic to any systematic codification of New Zealand law. There are no civil or criminal 'codes' and there are few statutes of a general and comprehensive nature. The statutes closest to that description would be the Crimes Act 1961[50] and the Bills of Exchange Act 1908.

43. The Government retains responsibility for the publication and availability of New Zealand law. The Office of the Clerk of the House of Representatives and Parliamentary Counsel have the responsibility for preparing and ensuring the publication, printing, distribution and sale of Acts and regulations. Provisions on these matters are contained in the Legislation Act 2012. Legislation is published individually in loose-leaf form, can be commercially printed on demand from the Parliamentary Counsel Office's website or found in annual collections. PDF copies of legislation published on the Parliamentary Counsel Office's website are official. Periodically, volumes of reprinted statutes with their amendments incorporated are issued. There has been no definitive collection of New Zealand legislation, though the reprinted collections of Statutes of 1908, 1931 and 1957 came close to achieving that. Nevertheless, the Legislation Act confirms the principle of Crown responsibility for making publicly available the text of enactments of the Legislature.[51]

44. Interpretation of statutes is aided by the Interpretation Act 1999. The courts will construe Acts according to their plain meaning wherever possible. Legislation is read subject to various common law interpretive conventions.[52]

§2. Hierarchy

45. The theory of parliamentary sovereignty which typifies the New Zealand constitutional position dictates the hierarchy of law in New Zealand. All enactments of the Parliament of New Zealand are equal. All can be as readily amended as each other. The exception to this is section 268 of the Electoral Act 1993.

---

50. However, New Zealand's criminal procedure law is no longer found in the Crimes Act 1961, but in the Criminal Procedure Act 2011.
51. *Victoria University of Wellington Students Association Inc. v. Shearer (Government Printer)* [1973] 2 NZLR 21.
52. The literal rule requires that statutes are given their ordinary meaning, the golden rule requires that statutes are interpreted so as to avoid absurdity. On these issues and statute law in New Zealand generally *see,* J.F. Burrows, *Statute Law in New Zealand* (4th ed., LexisNexis 2009). New legislation is free online at www.legislation.govt.nz and www.nzlii.org, and is also available to subscribers of Westlaw New Zealand and LexisNexis.

46. The next branch of legal rules is delegated legislation. Regulations and bylaws are not made by Parliament, but under authority delegated by Parliament in statutes to, for example, Ministers, local authorities and the Governor-General in Council. Such subsidiary legislation must be confined in its subject matter to the area authorized by the delegating statute. Failure to limit subsidiary legislation to the area authorized by the law may mean an application for judicial review. The High Court may strike down any subsidiary enactment made ultra vires the empowering statute, and any bylaw that is unreasonable.[53]

47. Statutes may be amended by regulations but only where there is a provision in the Act authorizing the amendment.[54]

48. Regulations may also be revoked by statute or, where the power exists to do so, by another regulation. In addition under the Legislation Act 2012, the House of Representatives may amend, revoke or substitute regulations by resolution. The individual Acts have different requirements for different regulations.

49. The status of judicial decisions in the legal hierarchy is harder to define. The doctrine of precedent obliges New Zealand courts to follow the decisions of courts of higher status than themselves; yet, the courts themselves are bound to interpret what Parliament enacts. They do not have the power to override statutes. Where no statute covers the area of law under consideration, then the case law is the ultimate authority. Decisions of the Privy Council relating to New Zealand law were till 2004 the supreme authority in the legal hierarchy. Since 2003 the Supreme Court is the top court in the New Zealand system.

50. This apparently clear-cut hierarchy of legal authority suggests that legislation is always supreme. Yet some authorities have challenged this supposition. Sir Robin Cooke, the former President of New Zealand's Court of Appeal has suggested that the courts have a role to play in determining the limits of Parliament's power.

In 1982, Sir Robin Cooke commented:

> we have reservations as to the extent to which in New Zealand even an Act of Parliament can take away the rights of citizens to resort to the ordinary Courts of law for the determination of their rights.[55]
>
> In 1984, he said:
>
> This is perhaps a reminder that it is arguable that some common law rights may go so deep that even Parliament cannot be accepted by the Courts to have destroyed them.[56]

---

53. For example, *see*, *Reade v. Smith* [1959] NZLR 996. On delegated legislation in New Zealand *see*, D.C. Pearce, *Delegated Legislation in Australia and New Zealand* (Butterworths 1977); and Ross Carter, Jason McHerron & Ryan Malone, *Subordinate Legislation in New Zealand* (Lexis Nexis 2013).
54. *Combined State Unions v. State Services Co-ordinating Committee* [1982] NZLR 742.
55. *New Zealand Drivers' Association v. New Zealand Road Carriers* [1982] 1 NZLR 374 at 390.
56. *Fraser v. State Services Commission* [1984] 1 NZLR 116 at 121.

and:

> I do not think that literal compulsion, by torture for instance, would be within the lawful powers of Parliament. Some common law rights presumably lie so deep that even Parliament could not override them.[57]

Sir Robin Cooke also observed:[58]

> My submission is that the modern common law should be seen to have a free and democratic society as its basic tenet and, for that reason, to be built on two complementary and lawfully unalterable principles: the operation of a democratic legislature and the operation of independent courts.
>
> I am suggesting that if a change, by legislation or otherwise, were seen to undermine either of them to a significant extent, it would be the responsibility of the Judges to say so and, if their judgments to that effect were disregarded, to resign or to acknowledge frankly that they are prepared to depart from their judicial oath and to serve a state not entitled to be called a free democracy.
>
> Suppose that an Act of the legislature purported to strip Jewish people of their citizenship and their property; or to disfranchise women (or men); or positively and without qualification to require the Courts, notwithstanding any rule of law to the contrary, to receive in evidence any statement appearing to be a confession of crime, whether or not obtained by force or any other form of compulsion. Can any lawyer in all honesty accept as a viable principle that some infringements of human rights are so grave that if enacted in other countries they will not be recognised as law at all by us, but that this would not matter if they were enacted by our own legislature?

This line of thought has, however, been rejected in Australia. Street J. while expressing an affinity for Sir Robin Cooke's views felt constrained by the absence of authority actually invalidating a statute and the authoritative rejection of such a doctrine by the House of Lords. Street J. preferred to rely on the constitutional restraints such as that of 'peace, welfare, and good government' as the authority for the courts to protect parliamentary democracy.[59] The President, Kirby P., agreed with Street J. commenting:

> Such extra-constitutional notions must be viewed with reservation not only because they lack the legitimacy that attaches to the enactments ultimately sanctioned by the people. But also because, once allowed, there is no logical limit to their ambit.[60]

---

57. *Taylor v. New Zealand Poultry Board* [1984] 1 NZLR 394 at 398. An article discussing this area is J.L. Caldwell, *Judicial Sovereignty – A New View*, NZLJ 357 (1984).
58. Rt Hon Sir Robin Cooke, *Fundamentals*, NZLJ 158, 164 (1988).
59. *Building Construction Employees and Builders' Labourers Federation of New South Wales v. Minister for Industrial Relations* (1986) 7 NSWLR 372, at 387.
60. *BLF v. Minister for Industrial Relations* (1986) 7 NSWLR 372, at 405. Kirby P.

Part II. Form of Government

Chapter 1. General

§1. Political Parties[61]

I. Introduction: Power of Governing Party

51. New Zealand's present political structure owes much to the country's heritage as a Colony and Dominion. The Westminster tradition inherited from Great Britain involved an electoral system of plurality voting for elected representatives on a geographical constituency basis. One result of this plurality voting system was the entrenchment in New Zealand's political history of a two-party system. It proved difficult for any third party to gain enough support to seriously affect the two-party balance of power within the Parliament.

Consequently, whichever party held the reins of government had a virtual monopoly on power within the Parliament. Voting in the legislative chamber was predominantly on party lines, so the Government could carry legislation through Parliament at will. The Government also had mastery in the sense that it controlled the procedural routine of Parliament: it advised the Governor-General on the summoning, dissolution and prorogation of Parliament; it controlled the business of Parliament on at least two out of three days and it appointed Select Committee members; it determined when debates should be ended or adjourned. Such mastery led to many calls for reform of the electoral system, and resulted in the appointment of the Royal Commission on the Electoral System, and the subsequent report in 1986,[62] which in turn led to the adoption from 1996 of a new electoral system based on proportional representation.

Despite its control in the legislature, the Government could not prevent Opposition criticism and delaying tactics, ploys that are vital to the effective operation of the House. It is here that the two-party system had some value, as problems with proposed legislation were pointed out, and possible amendments debated. In theory, the Government could also change the rules of Parliament, the Standing Orders of

61. A general reference text on politics in New Zealand is S. Levine, *The New Zealand Political System: Politics in a Small Society* (George Allen and Unwin 1979) and P. Harris & S. Levine, *The New Zealand Politics Source Book* (3d ed., Dunmore Press 1999). More recent texts include Richard Mulgan *Politics in New Zealand* (3d ed., Auckland U. Press 2003) and Raymond Miller (ed.), *New Zealand Government and Politics* (5th ed., Oxford U. Press, 2010).

62. *Report of the Royal Commission on the Electoral System: Towards a Better Democracy* (Government Printer, 1986). Also published in AJHR 1986, H.3.

the House, so as to stack Select Committees with Government representatives, refuse to allow Bills to be examined before Committees, refuse time for submissions to Committees, and end media coverage of parliamentary proceedings. However, the abuse of such time-honoured procedures would have almost certainly been perceived by the electorate as undemocratic and a governing party indulging in such tactics would soon find itself performing the duties of the Opposition. The concern with the reaction of the electorate was the most effective, and perhaps the only real curb on a Government with a healthy majority.

The implementation of the new system of voting may eventually see the cessation of the two-party system, and the re-emergence of the strength of Parliament. Under the MMP voting system no one party has yet had a majority. This makes it more difficult for legislation to be passed hastily.

Central government elections have been conducted since 1996 on an MMP basis. Under MMP voters have two votes, one for their preferred candidate in the electorate in which they live, and the other for the party of their choice. The use of this system has seen the introduction of a number of prominent minority parties, such as New Zealand First, ACT New Zealand, the Green Party, United Future and the Maori Party. The introduction of minority parties has resulted in coalition governments and agreements between a major party and some minority parties in order to achieve a parliamentary majority on matters of confidence and supply.

Following the 2014 election the National Party formed the minority government with agreements of confidence and supply with the Maori Party, ACT and United Future.

52. Political parties in New Zealand have evolved as part of the political process, rather than developing as separate from it. Party aspirations to political power have been largely confined to Parliament, rather than overflowing into community affairs. This is doubtless aided by the fact that, since 1876, New Zealand has had no provincial or federal system of government. Major political activity has been confined to the House of Representatives in Wellington. Until 1891, with the coming to power of the Liberal Government, permanent political alliances were unknown in New Zealand politics. However, the success of the Liberals forced the other members in the House of Representatives to organize themselves into an opposition party. This party was subsequently elected to government as the Reform Party in 1912, drawing support from established rural, commercial and industrial interests. The Reform Party espoused free enterprise principles to counteract the perceived socialist leanings of the Liberals whose support came from workers and small farmers.

Thus, party allegiances occurred inside Parliament, and parties grew outwards from the centre of political power into the community, as they sought an electoral base. It was not until the foundation of the Labour Party in 1916 that a political party in New Zealand had an efficient and effective extra-parliamentary support structure. Such organization showed its value when the Labour Party became the government in 1935.

The Opposition, the remnants of the Reform and United (Liberal) parties which had governed as a coalition from 1931 to 1935, saw the value of strong organization, and responded in kind with the establishment in 1936 of the National Party.

With a mass membership providing a broad voting base, the National Party quickly rose to become the second of the country's two major political parties, and achieved electoral success for the first time in 1949. Despite an abundance of minor parties which have achieved varying degrees of support, the National and Labour parties remain the dominant forces in New Zealand politics.

53. The Labour Party had its roots in the socialist radicalism of the early twentieth century, but was early forced to abandon its radicalism to avoid stagnation Nevertheless, it maintains links with the union movement. The loyalty of unions to the Labour Party declined somewhat following the 1984–1990 term of the Fourth Labour Government which accepted orthodox free-market monetarism. It was the reaction against this which helped bring about the defeat of the Labour Party in the General Election of 1990, and then the return of the Labour Party to more traditional labour policies of State interventionism and liberal humanitarianism.

54. National Party ideology reflects support of private enterprise, and of individualism in economic, social and political spheres of life. This ethic has traditionally appealed to farmers, the commercial sector and middle-class interests in general. In short, it may be said that the National Party is more right wing than the Labour Party. Increasingly, however, the middle ground in New Zealand society is where elections are won or lost. No longer can the two main parties claim to draw their support from any particular social groupings. Consequently, recent elections have seen both parties wooing voters from the same groups in order to achieve the majority needed to become the government.

55. Political parties are generally unincorporated societies, and are subject to very little law, regulation or conventions. They are free to regulate their own procedure and do so by their various constitutions. The 2014 Parliament has seven parliamentary parties: National Party, Labour Party, Green Party, New Zealand First, Maori Party, ACT New Zealand and United Future.

II. Registration of Political Parties

56. Pursuant to Part IV of the Electoral Act 1993, political parties which have at least 500 current financial members may apply for registration. Only those parties which are registered may submit party lists from which their list MPs are chosen.[63] Applications may be refused if the party has not complied with the application procedures or if the name of the party is unsatisfactory or misleading or if the party does not have the required 500 members.[64]

Applications for registration of a political party must be made in writing to the Electoral Commission, set out details concerning the party, and include a statutory

63. *See*, discussion on the new electoral system and list of MPs in paras 71–75.
64. Electoral Act 1993, ss 65 and 66.

declaration that the party has the required 500 members.[65] Registration may be cancelled if the number of financial members falls below 500.[66] The Act provides that registered parties must employ democratic procedures in candidate selection.[67]

III. Eligibility to Stand as Candidate

57. Only persons who are registered as electors are eligible to stand for Parliament either in a constituency or list seat.[68] A candidate must be a New Zealand citizen.[69]

State servants may not be candidates.[70] Those who wish to stand for election to Parliament are given leave of absence[71] and if elected the State servant is deemed to have vacated office as a State servant.[72]

IV. Party Organization within Parliament and Outside

58. The behaviour of Members of Parliament is governed by the Standing Orders of the House of Representatives and by the rules of the individual's party.

59. A Minister must be present during all sitting hours of the House of Representatives; otherwise, the Speaker should adjourn the House until the time for its next sitting.[73] Order in the House during debates is enforced by the Speaker of the House.[74] In this regard all members are treated equally in the House, that is, as if they were sitting purely as individually elected members.

60. When Parliament is not sitting, the difference in the procedures of both major parties with regard to the conduct of members is not marked. Both Government and Opposition Members of Parliament meet weekly in caucus meetings. The conduct of caucus meetings is determined by the rules of the individual party. Caucus meetings of both major parties are chaired by the parliamentary leader of the party and are conducted to establish a common party outlook on various questions. Perhaps the main consequence of caucus organization is the way it forces unanimity upon a party in the House. For example, upon successful nomination as the candidate for an electorate, Labour Party members sign a pledge which requires them

65. Section 63.
66. Section 70.
67. Section 71.
68. Electoral Act 1993, s. 47.
69. Section 47(3).
70. Section 48.
71. Section 52.
72. Section 53.
73. Standing Order 40.
74. Standing Order 84.

to vote in the House 'on all questions in accordance with the decisions of the Caucus of the Parliamentary Labour Party'.[75] This rigid line has forced dissident Labour MPs to resign from the party when they wished to express formal disagreement with the official party line. Whilst in theory there is more freedom for National Party members to cross the floor and vote contrary to official party policy, in reality this is not often done. National Party candidates agree to abide by the party's Rules and Constitution and to be loyal to the party leader. As the party leader and Cabinet set the standard in Caucus, voting against the National Party line will usually be contrary to the required loyalty to the party leader.

61. Outside Parliament, party organization is entirely in the hands of the parties themselves.

62. When the National Party was formed it wished to build a large base of electoral support rapidly, and so opened its membership to anyone who wished to join. Since then, despite membership fluctuations, the National Party has retained a very broad-based membership approach, and this is the base from which its electoral support is drawn. Due in part to the laxity of its membership rules, the parliamentary National Party and the extra-parliamentary party remain largely separate. The latter is concerned with fund-raising, building up membership and electioneering, and the former with conducting parliamentary affairs. There is some overlap between the two wings of the party in terms of formulating policy, yet the extra-parliamentary National Party has less involvement in policy than its Labour Party counterpart.
The National Party meets on four distinct levels: branch, electorate, regional and national. The essential duty of branch committees is to enrol members and collect membership subscriptions and funds. Branch committees operate within electorates. Electorate committees are made up either of representatives elected by branch committees (including Young Nationals, the youth wing of the party) or of party members of the electorate elected at an annual meeting. Electorate committees have the functions of enrolling members, arranging the selection of constituency candidates for elections, providing funding and organization for the election of candidates, and raising funds and conducting political and social activities in their electorate. Electorates are grouped into regions to assist each other and coordinate local policy consultation. Each region holds an annual conference, where policy may be debated. There is also an annual national conference, primarily comprised of delegates from electorates, where the policy of the party is considered. Annual conferences also elect the members of the Board of Directors, which governs the affairs of the party, and in theory can change the party constitution.

Selection of constituency candidates is the responsibility of the electorates. However, the Board of Directors has an unfettered discretion to approve or disapprove any candidates for selection.

The leader of the party, who will most likely be the Prime Minister if the National Party attains the highest vote in a General Election, is appointed as soon as practicable after each General Election by the members of the Party elected to the House of Representatives (known as the Parliamentary Section).

75. New Zealand Labour Party Constitution and Rules 2014, Art. 300.

Such a combination of higher and lower level decision-making is typical of National Party compromise.

63. Organizationally, the Labour Party is structured around electorate committees which are grouped into regional councils. The electorate committees comprise delegates from affiliated unions and branch members, who in turn send representatives to six annual regional functions, thus providing feedback and communication channels between members and parliamentarians. At the annual Labour Party Conference nearly all the members of the Executive and about half of the New Zealand Council are elected. In addition, the conference elects five members to the sixteen-person Policy Council. This body has the final say in determining the Party's election manifesto. In practice, however, there is considerable interaction between the New Zealand Council, caucus and the Policy Council itself. Remits passed by the Labour Party conference are also treated more seriously by the policy makers than is the case in the National Party.

Candidate selection in the Labour Party is influenced by the Party leadership. Candidates are selected by a Selection Committee comprised of three members of the New Zealand Council, one or two members of the local electorate committee depending on the strength of the local electorate committee's organization, and one local Party members' representative elected by and from local Party members present at the selection meeting. One selection vote is gained following a secret ballot amongst eligible party members present at the selection meeting. This gives considerable scope to the party hierarchy to reject disloyal or dissident candidates, because if local opinion is divided, as it often is, then a united New Zealand Council representation vote will usually ensure selection of its chosen candidate.

64. Under MMP, parties also select list candidates. Each party sets its own rules for the selection of its list candidates, subject to the requirement that the candidates be democratically elected.

65. In theory, there is nothing to stop any individual who meets the requirements of the Electoral Act 1993 as to candidacy from forming a political party or standing as an independent candidate and running for political office. However, the reality of the current voting system in New Zealand is that such a candidate's chances of success are very slim. No candidate standing as an independent has sat in the New Zealand Parliament since 1946.[76]

Under the pre-1996 system, minor parties if they achieved any seats at all, usually achieved a far lower proportion of seats than the percentage of the vote obtained.[77] Such uneven distribution prompted many calls for reform.

76. Though in recent years MPs have sat as independents after leaving their political parties once elected.

77. In 1995, four seats in the House were held by third parties elected under a third-party banner. Two of those seats were held by the Alliance, which had obtained 17.21% of the vote, and two were held by New Zealand First, which had obtained 8.40% of the vote.

66. In 1986, the Royal Commission[78] (which had been convened to consider the fairness of the system) delivered a comprehensive report, addressing what it perceived to be the inadequacies in the New Zealand electoral system. As well as resolving the problem of unfair distribution of seats in the House, the Commission sought to redress the low representation of women and racial minorities in the political system. Much of the report was concerned with assessing viable alternatives to the plurality system. The Commission recommended the adoption in New Zealand of a representation system similar to that used in Germany.[79]

The Royal Commission also considered the possibility of re-establishing an Upper House or Senate for New Zealand.[80] New Zealand has not had an Upper House since the Legislative Council was abolished in 1950.[81] The Royal Commission did not favour the establishment of a second chamber. Although recognizing the need for constitutional safeguards to prevent the abuse by the House of Representatives of its considerable powers, the Commission felt other safeguards were more appropriate than an Upper House and that developments within New Zealand in the preceding decade towards more open and accountable government had in many cases dealt with any problems that might be met by an Upper House. These developments included the promulgation of the Official Information Act 1982,[82] the establishment of the Human Rights Commission[83] and the increased review of legislation by Select Committees.[84] In addition the Commission felt that any benefits to be gained in the representation of under-represented minority groups by a second chamber would be better achieved by instituting a new electoral system. The new system is discussed later in this chapter.

§2. Lobbies and Interest Groups

67. New Zealand is not a State where governmental power lies purely within sectional interest groups. Nevertheless, there is considerable scope for the proliferation of interest groups to influence government direction by means of the consultative process. There is an abundance of interest groups in New Zealand, all eager to safeguard their rights and see Government policy progress in the direction they

78. *Report of the Royal Commission on the Electoral System: Towards a Better Democracy* (Government Printer, 1986). Also published in AJHR 1986, H.3.
79. Paragraphs 2.116 and 2.179. The system is now in place and is discussed below.
80. Paragraphs 9.151 to 9.156.
81. Legislative Council Abolition Act 1950.
82. Providing for official information to be made more freely available.
83. The Human Rights Commission was originally constituted under s. 4 of the Human Rights Commission Act 1977. That Act was repealed by the Human Rights Act 1993. The Human Rights Commission is continued under s. 4 of the 1993 Act.
84. The Regulations Review Committee scrutinizes delegated legislation (promulgated and in draft form) to ensure for example that the legislation is in conformity with the intentions of the parent Act. Alongside Select Committees, there are other bodies which scrutinize legislation, such as the Legislation Advisory Committee. That Committee was established in 1986 and its members are appointed by the Minister of Justice. Its functions are to advise the Government and Parliament on legislative proposals. A further development was the appointment of Ombudsmen pursuant to the Ombudsmen Act 1975. The function of the Ombudsmen is to investigate complaints against Government departments in regard to their administrative decisions or recommendations.

desire. Such groups range from financial, professional and trade interests, through to recreational, social and religious groups. They attempt to influence Government policy and to influence the Government decision-making process. This may be achieved either by gaining formal recognition as an advice-giver, or by making representations informally to the Government.

68. Formal recognition of interest groups arises in a variety of ways. Independent bodies may be recognized statutorily or given delegated power by statute. Thus, for example, the Royal Society of New Zealand Act 1997 establishes a body for 'the advancement and promotion in New Zealand of science, technology and the humanities'.[85] The Act is a Private Act,[86] but the Society is exempt from taxation.[87] Other bodies, which are not necessarily statutorily incorporated, are also given funds by the Government for the performance of specific tasks. Examples are the Automobile Association and Federated Farmers. In this way the Government recognizes a group's authority within a certain area, and recognizes its contribution to administration in that area. A group may also be recognized as the only channel to which the Government will dispense information. Thus, in wage-fixing the Government may be prepared to negotiate only with one organization. This organization will probably be the most broadly based and representative available.

69. At a less formal level, some interest groups simply organize themselves as best they can to influence Government. Typically they make submissions to Select Committees on matters that concern them, and thus share to some extent in the legislative process. They also keep in contact with Government departments so that their concerns are not unknown to the government. Some groups, especially those concerned with single issues, seek to achieve a high public profile and carry public opinion with them on that issue. Such organizations are less closely linked to Government processes than other groups.

70. Perhaps the most effective way of keeping a group's interests before the government is to employ a fulltime lobbyist, or for an organization member to have the task of maintaining a high organizational profile before the Government. It is usually only large groups which are able to maintain this level of activity. Such groups include large industrial groupings like the Council of Trade Unions and the Employers and Manufacturers Association.

§3. Electoral Reform 1993

71. Until 1994, the New Zealand electoral system was a 'first-past-the-post' system which was governed by the Electoral Act 1956. Essentially the Act divided the

85. Section 5.
86. Section 41.
87. Clause 11 of the Schedule.

country into constituencies on the basis of population.[88] At an election, the candidate who received the most votes in each constituency was elected as that constituency's Member of Parliament.

This system was relatively simple. However, it helped perpetuate an arrangement by which two major parties dominated the House of Representatives.[89]

72. When the Royal Commission reported in 1986, it recommended the adoption of the MMP system of voting as used in the then Federal Republic of Germany.[90] MMP was favoured over the Single Transferable Vote, Supplementary Member and Preferential Voting systems. MMP was seen to guarantee a closer connection between votes received and seats in the Parliament, and the Royal Commission also believed it would result in the election of more women and Members of Parliament from racial minorities.

73. The Electoral Referendum Act 1991 provided for a referendum on the electoral system.[91] Electors were asked, first, whether they wished to retain the 'first-past-the-post' system or whether they would prefer a changed voting system and, second, if the system was changed whether it should change to the Preferential Voting (PV), MMP, Supplementary Member System (SM), or single transferable vote (STV) system of voting.[92]

The poll was to be indicative only, but the result sent the Government a clear signal that many New Zealanders desired change. Although only 55.2% of voters voted in the referendum, 84.7% of valid votes cast were in favour of change. Of those who answered the second question, 70.5% indicated a preference for MMP.

Subsequently, a binding referendum was held concurrently with the 1993 General Election. Voters were then asked to choose between the 'first-past-the-post' and MMP systems. A majority of votes for MMP would bring the MMP system into operation on 1 July 1994. The MMP option won the poll with 53.8% of the votes.

74. As recommended by the Royal Commission, the Electoral Act 1993 provides for an increase in the number of MPs to approximately 120.[93] About half of these are elected on a constituency basis, with the population of the South Island divided into sixteen electorates and the North Island allotted electorates according to the number of voters in South Island electorates.[94] The number of Maori electoral districts likewise depends on the size of the other electorates and the number

---

88. In 1993, there were ninety-nine constituencies, with the number of South Island constituencies fixed at twenty-five and those in the North Island being adjusted as the North Island population grew in proportion to the South Island population.
89. A party might receive 20.7% of the vote nationwide yet only *see*, two MPs returned (as happened in 1981), or, as occurred in 1984, a party might receive 12.3% of the vote without gaining any seats.
90. *Report of the Royal Commission on the Electoral System* (*see, above*).
91. Section 3 and Schedule.
92. The referendum was held on 19 Sep. 1992. *See also*, the Electoral Referendum Act 1993 and the Electoral Referendum Act 2010 where further electoral referendum were provided for.
93. Section 191.
94. Section 35.

of voters on the Maori electoral roll.[95] The remaining seats will be filled from candidates listed on pre-arranged party lists.[96] Voters have one vote for their constituency MP and another vote for a registered political party. Parties are awarded list seats to redress any imbalance between the number of constituency seats they win and the overall percentage of the party vote that they receive.[97]

Thus, a party which wins one constituency seat but gains 10% of the overall party vote is awarded an extra eleven seats to give it twelve seats – that is the 10% of the 120 seats to which the party vote entitles it. The Act sets a threshold at 5% so that no seats will be awarded to a party which achieves less than 5% of the party vote unless that party also has a constituency Member of Parliament elected.[98]

75. The Electoral Act 1993 requires that candidates on party lists be democratically selected by the financial members of the party.[99] These lists must then be available to voters before the election so that they can see whom their party vote may put into office. It is permissible for a candidate to stand for a constituency seat and also to be on the party list, although, if elected to a constituency, that candidate's name will be removed from the party list when the time comes for allocating list seats.[100]

§4. Popular Initiatives: Petitions and the Like

76. Provision is made under Chapter 7 of the Standing Orders of the House of Representatives 2014 for the presentation of petitions to the House. Provided that a petition meets the requirements of Standing Orders, any person may present one. Such requirements relate to tone and procedure. Petitions are an avenue by which petitioners seek a redress of a grievance, whether through an alteration to the law, or a change in an administrative decision. Once drawn up and completed, a petition is given to a Member of Parliament for presentation in the House.[101] Members must ensure that petitions conform to the Standing Orders of the House, which as well as requiring conformity with the rules of presentation also require that petitioners have exhausted their legal remedies or where applicable gone to the Ombudsman and that the petition does not concern an issue with which the House has previously dealt.[102] After presentation, the Clerk of the House distributes the petition to a Select Committee for consideration and report.

95. Section 45.
96. Sections 127 and 191–193.
97. Section 191.
98. Section 191(4). This quota is valid for any party that wins a constituency seat. A party that wins one constituency seat and receives 4% of the party vote will be awarded list seats to give it 4% of the overall parliamentary representation.
99. Section 71.
100. Section 193(3).
101. Standing Order 369.
102. Standing Order 371.

This process is an important part of New Zealand's democratic processes. Although there is no guarantee that a petition will meet with any success, the possibility remains that it will achieve something. Petitions are a check on the political process. The petition process is also used by interest groups to generate public interest and action on particular issues.

All petitions that appear before Select Committees are reported in the Appendix to the Journals of the House of Representatives. Numerous petitions have been presented to the House over the years. Examples are the 1893 petition for women's suffrage[103] and the petition in 1970 objecting to the raising of the level of Lake Manapouri.[104]

§5. REFERENDA

77. Three types of referendum are possible in New Zealand. The first is electoral referenda. Under the Electoral Act 1993 certain provisions of the Constitution Act 1986 and the Electoral Act 1993 are entrenched. In order to amend or repeal these provisions it is necessary to gain either a 75% majority in the House of Representatives or a majority of valid votes cast in a poll of electors from the general and Maori electoral districts. These provisions relate to the term of Parliament, the Representation Commission, electoral districts, the electoral quota, the voting age and method of voting.[105]

Over the years four electoral referenda have been held. In 1967, legislation was passed to enable a referendum on proposals to extend the parliamentary term to four years.[106] Again in 1990,[107] the same proposal was put again. In neither case was the majority required for change attained. These were not binding referenda. A 75% majority in Parliament would still have been needed to make the changes to the law.

In 1992, a further non-binding electoral referendum was held to ascertain whether voters desired a change to the voting system.[108]

The most significant referendum was the binding 1993 referendum held in conjunction with the general election, on the voting system.[109]

More recently, a non-binding electoral referendum was held on the voting system in 2011 in conjunction with the general election. It asked two questions: first whether New Zealand should retain the MMP voting system, and second which voting system voters would choose if New Zealand were to change to another voting system.[110] 56.17% of voters chose to keep MMP. Due to that result, there was an independent review of MMP in 2012 to recommend any changes that should be made to the system.

103. 1893 JHR Schedule of Petitions Presented xvii.
104. 1970 JHR Schedule of Petitions Presented 583.
105. Section 268. *See,* earlier discussion.
106. Electoral Poll Act 1967.
107. Term Poll Act 1990.
108. Electoral Referendum Act 1991. *See,* earlier discussion.
109. Electoral Referendum Act 1993. *See,* earlier discussion.
110. Electoral Referendum Act 2010.

78. The second type of referendum is one initiated under the Citizens Initiated Referenda Act 1993. This Act provides for petitions to be presented to the House of Representatives asking for an indicative referendum on a particular issue.[111] Proposals for petitions are submitted to the Clerk of the House who publishes the proposal in the *New Zealand Gazette*.[112] The final wording of the question is decided by the Clerk of the House.[113] A form is approved for use for collection of signatures.[114] Notice of approval is given to the person submitting the proposal and to the public.[115] The promoter of the petition may then proceed to promote the petition and gather the necessary signatures. The promoter has twelve months within which to gather the required signatures or it will lapse. The petition is then authenticated by the Clerk of the House to ensure that it has been signed by 10% of eligible voters and that all signatures are valid.[116] It is then presented to the Speaker of the House[117] and a date or voting period for the referendum is appointed by the Governor-General in Council.[118] The referendum is then held as if it was an electoral poll,[119] or by postal voting.[120]

There have been four recent citizens initiated referenda of significance. The results of the referenda were not binding on the Government: In 1999, there was a petition to reduce the number of MPs from 120 to 99. 81.5% of voters voted to reduce the number of MPs. There was no change in the number of MPs.

In 1999, there was also a referendum asking 'Should there be a reform of the justice system placing greater emphasis on the needs of victims, providing restitution and compensation for them and imposing minimum sentences and hard labour for all serious violent offences?' Ninety-two per cent of voters voted yes. The Sentencing Act was passed in 2002. One of the purposes of this Act is 'to provide for the interests of victims of crimes'.

In 2008, there was a referendum asking 'Should a smack as part of good parental correction be a criminal offence in New Zealand?' The referendum came about in response to a 2007 Bill which would amend the Crimes Act 1961 to remove parental correction as a defence for an assault against a child and 87.4% of voters answered no to the question. The Bill had already passed into law before the referendum was held. The Government took the view that the amendment has been working well, and took no action in response to the referendum.

In 2013, in response to a 2011 announcement by the Government that it would partially privatize four State-owned enterprises and reduce its share in Air New Zealand, there was a referendum asking 'Do you support the Government selling up to 49% of Meridian Energy, Mighty River Power, Genesis Power, Solid Energy and Air New Zealand? And 67.3% of voters answered no. Following the result, the

111. Sections 3 and 5.
112. Sections 6 and 7.
113. Section 11.
114. Section 12.
115. Section 13.
116. Sections 18 and 19.
117. Section 18.
118. Section 22.
119. Sections 22(2)(a). 22AA and 24.
120. Sections 22(2)(b), 22AB and 24A.

Prime Minister announced the asset sales programme would continue, as he said the Government was re-elected in 2011 partially on the basis of the asset sales policy.

79. The third type of referendum is Government-initiated conscience referenda. There have been a variety of such referenda over the years, typically on matters of national importance. The most significant were the liquor referenda which were conducted at the same time as general elections from 1893 to 1987. The polls were set up under the Alcoholic Liquors Sale Control Act 1893. Each parliamentary electorate was made a licensing district. At the poll electors voted on licensing in their area. By 1911, 56% of voters supported prohibition but a 60% majority was needed to carry the vote. Since then the vote for prohibition steadily decreased.

Another referendum of note was held on 9 March 1949. It was on the issue of off-course betting on horse races.[121] A further referendum in that year related to compulsory military training.[122]

80. Whether the result of a referendum is binding on the Government depends on the law which empowers the holding of the referendum. Electoral referenda are binding on the Government. The Royal Commission felt that all referenda should carry some weight and be more than purely indicative.[123] It was felt that, if a certain percentage of the electorate (e.g., two-thirds) voted on the question, then the Government should feel morally bound to enact legislation to put the people's wishes into effect. Alternatively, Bills before the House could contain clauses requiring a majority vote of two-thirds turn out in favour before they become law.

---

121. *New Zealand Gazette 1949*, vol. I, 86[illegible]. The majority of voters in the poll favoured off-course betting.
122. *New Zealand Gazette 1949*, vol. II, 1784. The majority favoured compulsory military training.
123. Paragraph 7.31.

Chapter 2. Head of State

§1. The Sovereign

81. New Zealand is a constitutional monarchy with a Queen or King as its Head of State.[124] However, the Head of State does not govern the country. Although representative of the power of the State and of national identity, the Monarch is by convention bound to follow the advice of responsible Ministers and acts only on the advice of those Ministers. In her role as Queen of New Zealand, Queen Elizabeth II acts through her representative, the Governor-General. The official title of the Queen of New Zealand (which applies also for New Zealand's associated States of the Cook Islands and Niue) is 'Elizabeth the Second, by the Grace of God Queen of New Zealand and Her Other Realms and Territories, Head of the Commonwealth, Defender of the Faith.'[125]

§2. The Crown

82. The Sovereign and the Crown are often used interchangeably. However, the Crown encompasses not only the Sovereign but also the Government. The Crown is a symbol of the State of New Zealand. It is a corporation sole and the source of all legal authority within New Zealand. It is by this authority that the Government acts.[126]

§3. The Royal Prerogative[127]

83. There are a number of powers enjoyed by the Sovereign and the Crown which are necessary for the running of government. These special prerogatives are generally rights and powers but may also encompass privileges and immunities, and are not typical of those which exist between private individuals.

The prerogative dates back to the time of the King as a superior body. Over time it was subject to restraints. For example, the *Case of Proclamations*[128] held that a royal proclamation forbidding new buildings in London area was unlawful. The Bill

124. Section 2 of the Constitution Act 1986 states that 'The Sovereign in right of New Zealand is the head of State of New Zealand, and shall be known by the royal style and titles proclaimed from time to time.' The use of the term 'in right of New Zealand' distinguishes New Zealand from the other monarchies for which the UK sovereign is Head of State.

125. Royal Titles Act 1974, s. 2.

126. The Crown has been defined to include: 'the Sovereign as Head of State in right of each of the Commonwealth countries; the Sovereign's personal representative, the Governor-General; ministers of the Crown inside and outside Cabinet; the Executive Council which formally advises the Sovereign or her representative, the Governor-General; the central government departments that execute the legal powers and policy directives of Ministers, and a range of closely controlled public bodies that qualify as instruments of executive government'. (P.A. Joseph, *Constitutional and Administrative Law in New Zealand* 622 (4th ed., Thomson Brookers 2014).

127. For a full discussion on the Royal Prerogative *see,* Joseph, Ch. 18.

128. (1611) 12 Co Rep 74.

of Rights 1688[129] curtailed some abuses of the Royal prerogative. Some of the more important prerogatives which may belong to the Sovereign personally or to the Crown generally are:

(i) *The King can do no wrong:*[130]
This encompasses two ideas – that the King being a supreme body can do no wrong and that the King cannot be sued in his own Courts. This effectively meant that the King could do and authorize no wrong and could not be sued in a personal capacity for public or private acts or torts committed by Ministers acting for the Crown. This is quite clearly still the principle – the Sovereign cannot be sued in a personal capacity – but statutes such as the Crown Proceedings Act 1950 do impose liability on the Crown. Pursuant to that Act, any person may enforce civil proceedings against the Crown in respect of breaches of contract, tortious acts and various other causes of action.[131] Proceedings are held in the same manner as proceedings between 'subject and subject'[132] and the Court may generally grant the types of relief which could be granted in a case between 'subjects'.[133]

(ii) *Crown not bound by statutes:*
This encompasses the idea that the Crown is not bound by a statute except by express words in the statute or by necessary implication. This principle exists at common law[134] and was codified in New Zealand in the Interpretation Act 1999.[135]

(iii) *The Royal revenues:*
The Sovereign is generally exempt from taxation. This privilege also applies to the Governor-General of New Zealand whose salary, which is payable out of public money without further appropriation, is exempt from income tax.[136]

(iv) *The right to be consulted:*
This involves the right of the Sovereign to be kept informed on affairs of the nation and other matters. This right is also enjoyed by the Governor-General.[137]

---

129. 1 Will and Mar, Sess 2, Ch. 2.
130. Joseph, 662–665.
131. Sections 3 and 6.
132. Section 12.
133. Section 17. However, the Court cannot grant injunction, order for specific performance, order for recovery of land or delivery of property against the Crown: s. 17(1). The Court's power in responding to requests for satisfaction of orders against the Crown is restricted to issuing a certificate of judgment certifying judgment debt: s. 24.
134. *Gorton Local Board v. Prison Commissioners (Note)* [1904] 2 KB 165; *Province of Bombay v. Municipal Corporation of Bombay* [1947] AC 58; *cf. Bropho v. Western Australia* (1990) 171 CLR 1; Joseph, 666–678.
135. Section 27; *Hohepa Wi Neera v. Bishop of Wellington* (1902) 21 NZLR 655; *Re Buckhingham* [1922] NZLR 771; *McDougall v. Attorney-General* [1925] NZLR 104.
136. Governor-General Act 2010, ss 5, 12 and 23; Joseph, 660–661.
137. Letters Patent, clause XVI; Joseph, 661–662.

(v) *The Sovereign never dies:*
The idea that the Sovereign never dies is a reflection of the Sovereign's supremacy. In practice the death of a Sovereign did have practical implications: Parliament was dissolved and legal actions discontinued. In 1908, the Demise of the Crown Act held that Parliament would continue despite the Sovereign's demise and preserved various Crown proceedings. That Act was repealed by the Constitution Act 1986 which provides:[138] 'The death of the Sovereign shall have the effect of transferring all the functions, duties, powers, authorities, rights, privileges, and dignities belonging to the Sovereign's successor, as determined in accordance with the enactment of the Parliament of England intituled The Act of Settlement (12 & 13 Will 3, c2) and any other law relating to the succession to the Throne, but shall otherwise have no effect in law for any purpose.'

(vi) *Legislative powers*:
   (a) Pursuant to the Royal prerogative the Sovereign may summon, prorogue and dissolve Parliament.[139]
   (b) The Royal assent is needed before any Act becomes law. It is unlikely that the Governor-General would refuse to assent to a law.[140]

(vii) *Appointments.*
The Sovereign is responsible, on the advice of the Ministers, for appointments to a range of positions in the Government, the judiciary and to public office generally. Pursuant to the Letters Patent of 1983,[141] this responsibility is delegated to the Governor-General of New Zealand who appoints people to a wide range of positions encompassing Ministers, judges, Royal Commissions, diplomatic representatives and other public offices.

(viii) *Honours.*
The Sovereign alone may dispense honours. In New Zealand honours are conferred by the Sovereign on the advice of the Prime Minister.[142]

(ix) *Armed forces.*
The command of the armed forces is vested in the Sovereign. The Governor-General, as the Sovereign's representative in New Zealand is, pursuant to the Letters Patent of 1983, the Commander-in-Chief of the armed forces.[143]

(x) *Statutes and the prerogative.*
A statute may expressly abolish or preserve an area of prerogative and impose a new rule. Where no express intention is made clear it is unlikely that the court would hold that the prerogative was excluded by implication. However, in certain cases the prerogative may be suspended by the statute, and the repeal of that statute is unlikely to revive the prerogative.[144]

---

138. Section 5(1); Joseph 662.
139. Constitution Act 1986, s. 18; *see also,* Letters Patent, clause III; Joseph, 701–702.
140. Joseph, 702–703.
141. Clause X; Joseph, 686–688.
142. Joseph, 699–701.
143. Clauses I, II; Defence Act 1990, s. 6; Joseph, 690–693.
144. *Attorney-General v. De Keyser's Royal Hotel Ltd* [1920] AC 508; Joseph, 674–678. For current discussion on prerogatives *see, R (Bancoult) v. Secretary of State for Foreign and Commonwealth Affairs* (No. 2) [2008] UKHL 61.

§4. THE GOVERNOR-GENERAL

I. Legal Status

84. The Sovereign's personal representative in New Zealand is the Governor-General.[145] The Governor-General is appointed by the Sovereign and carries out similar duties in New Zealand as are performed by the Queen in the United Kingdom.

85. When New Zealand was established as a Crown Colony, a Governor was appointed as head of the local administration, with considerable freedom to act as he or she saw fit. With the passing of the New Zealand Constitution Act in 1852,[146] New Zealand gained 'responsible government', and the convention developed that the Governor was to follow the advice of his or her Ministers on all matters of government.

86. The Governor's job description was at first set out in the Commission and Royal Instructions presented to each Governor.

The first permanent Letters Patent and Royal Instructions appointing a Governor were issued in 1879.[147] Further Letters were issued in 1892 and 1907. In 1917, a further set of Letters Patent was issued.[148] The Letters Patent and Royal Instructions of 1907 reflected the new status of New Zealand as a Dominion and the Governor was re-designated as Governor-General. No further Letters were issued until 1983.[149]

By 1983 changes were needed to modernize the office of Governor-General.[150] The 1917 Letters Patent allowed the Governor-General to reject the advice of Ministers in certain circumstances; this was deleted from the 1983 Letters.

In 2006, the 1983 Letters Patent were amended. The 2006 amendment purports to modernize the language of the Oath of Office, update the references to the Office of Administrator because of the establishment of the Supreme Court, and allow the Governor-General to travel abroad without permission of the Sovereign and the members of the Executive Council to meet by modern telecommunication means.[151] Apart from responses to particular technological changes, it may also indicate the development of greater recognition within the Realm of the individuality of each of the members of the Realm and of the continuing weakening of the

145. Constitution Act 1986, s. 2.
146. 15 and 16 Vict, Ch. 72.
147. Royal Letters of Appointment.
148. *See, New Zealand Gazette* 24 Apr. 1919, vol. I, 1213–1215.
149. SR 1983/225 as amended by SR 1987/8 and SR2006/219.
150. *See,* A. Quentin-Baxter, *A Review of the Letters Patent 1917 Constituting the Office of Governor-General of New Zealand* (Cabinet Office 1980); F.M. Brookfield, *The Reconstituted Office of Governor-General*, NZLJ 256 (1985).
151. Letters Patent (2006) Amending Letters Patent Constituting the Office of Governor-General of New Zealand (SR 2006/219), Preamble.

prerogative in favour of the democratically elected representatives of the several countries.[152]

87. The Letters Patent of 1983 constitute the office of Governor-General of New Zealand, the Cook Islands, Niue, Tokelau and the Ross Dependency.[153] The Governor-General is empowered to exercise executive authority on behalf of New Zealand, directly or through officers.[154]

88. The Letters Patent establish an Executive Council, specifying its membership and quorum.[155] A number of powers and authorities are given to the Governor-General, for example to appoint members of the Executive Council[156] and to exercise the prerogative of mercy.[157] The Letters also specify that the Governor-General be kept informed of government matters by Ministers of the Crown[158] and aided and assisted by Ministers and other officers.[159]

89. In the absence of the Governor-General, provision is made for a senior member of the judiciary to be appointed Administrator of Government.[160] Under the Constitution Act 1986,[161] every power conferred on the Governor-General by or under any Act is a royal power exercisable on behalf of the Sovereign.[162]

90. The Governor-General must follow the advice of the Ministers of Government in all but the most exceptional of circumstances. This convention has been formalized by the Constitution Act 1986, which states that 'every reference in any Act to the Governor-General in Council or any other like expression includes a reference to the Sovereign acting by and with the advice and consent of the Executive Council'.[163]

91. Over the years the office of Governor-General has often been held by a New Zealander. This tendency was confirmed in 1977 by a government decision that as a further step towards national maturity, future Governors-General would be selected from New Zealanders living in New Zealand.[164]

The practice until 1930 was for an appointment to the post of Governor-General to be made by the Sovereign on the advice of the United Kingdom government after

152. For more detailed discussion, *see*, Tony Angelo, *The Letters Patent*, NZLJ 5 (2007).
153. Clause I.
154. Clause III.
155. Clauses VII–IX.
156. Clause X.
157. Clause XI.
158. Clause XVI.
159. Clause XVII.
160. Clause XII.
161. Section 3.
162. Examples of Acts conferring powers are the Judicature Act 1908 and the Electoral Act 1993.
163. Section 3.
164. The Governor-General in 2015 is Lieutenant-General Rt Hon Sir Jeremiah Mateparae GNZM QSO; he was formerly Chief of the New Zealand Defence Force and Director of the Government Communications Security Bureau.

consultation with the New Zealand Government. After the 1930 Imperial Conference appointments have been made on the recommendation of the relevant Commonwealth Government.[165]

92. It is essential to the holding of the position that the Governor-General acts in a non-partisan way, holding himself or herself and the office above the country's politics. The Governor-General must be seen by the country to be impartial.

II. Duties and Powers

93. The Governor-General performs three main sets of functions – ceremonial, symbolic and constitutional.

94. In the ceremonial function, the Governor-General acts as Head of State. He or she officiates at the opening of Parliament each year, conducts investitures, receives the credentials of diplomats accredited to New Zealand, is Commander-in-Chief of the New Zealand armed forces and receives visiting Heads of State. These ceremonial and social duties are what most bring the office into the public eye.

95. The second function of the Governor-General's office has been described as providing a unifying influence.[166] It is to embody the values of the nation – above political party and politics. This means attending many public functions, making speeches and generally 'meeting and greeting as broad a cross-section of the New Zealand community as possible'.[167]

96. The third function of the office is a constitutional one. As the Governor-General represents the Sovereign, government legally revolves around this office. It includes:

- chairing the Executive Council;
- giving the Royal assent to Bills;
- convoking, dissolving and proroguing Parliament;
- making formal appointments of a constitutional nature.

97. The Governor-General chairs the Executive Council[168] which is made up of all the Ministers of Government. It is a purely formal body; it meets every Monday to carry out its functions of making official appointments, passing regulations and

165. Joseph, 123–124.
166. Sir D. Blundell, *Some Reflections upon the Office of Governor-General in New Zealand*, 10 VUWLR 197 (1980).
167. Palmer, 25.
168. *See*, earlier discussion. The quorum for the Executive Council is specified in Clause IX of the Letters Patent Constituting the Office of the Governor-General of New Zealand: 'The Executive Council shall not proceed to the despatch of business unless two Members at the least (exclusive of any Member presiding in the absence of Our Governor-General) be present throughout the whole of the meeting at which any such business is despatched.'

other subsidiary legislation, and advising on the exercise of the prerogative of mercy. Decisions and laws made by the Executive Council[169] are said to be made by the authority of the Governor-General in Council.

98. The Governor-General's office provides the legal authority for Bills passed by the House of Representatives to become law, by giving the royal assent. The Constitution Act 1986 provides: 'A Bill passed by the House of Representatives shall become law when the Sovereign or the Governor-General assents to it and signs it in token of such assent.'[170]

99. Each session of Parliament is brought to an end by the exercise of the powers vested in the Governor-General. The issuing of the proclamation brings the House sittings to an end. The House cannot meet following its prorogation till Parliament is once again summoned to meet by the Governor-General. The Governor-General issues the proclamation dissolving the Parliament in being, and summons the new Parliament to convene no later than six weeks after the return of the writs for the general election.[171]

100. After a general election, the leader of the political party which obtains the majority of seats in the House of Representatives is invited by the Governor-General to become Prime Minister and to form the new government. The basis on which that invitation is made (that the person concerned commands majority support in the House) renders formal confirmation by the House of Representatives unnecessary.

The new Prime Minister forms a government by choosing party colleagues to hold office as Ministers and advises the Governor-General to appoint them accordingly. These Ministers who then largely make up Cabinet tender advice to the Governor-General in Council. The Governor-General also appoints Judges, Commissioners and certain other officers as required by legislation.

101. In all these matters the Governor-General obeys the central constitutional convention concerning the monarchy, that is, that the Sovereign must exercise the powers of the office on the advice of responsible Ministers.

102. Nevertheless, there are a few rare and controversial occasions when the Governor-General may not follow this convention.[172] These powers are the reserve powers which give the Governor-General a residual discretion. The precise content of the powers is unknown. However, such powers could conceivably be exercised:[173] (i) to refuse a request to dissolve Parliament; (ii) to dismiss a Prime Minister who has lost majority support in the House; (iii) to appoint a Prime Minister

169. Orders in Council.
170. Section 16.
171. Constitution Act 1986, ss 18 and 19.
172. An example is the dismissal of the Whitlam Ministry in Australia in 1975 by the Governor-General Sir John Kerr: Palmer, 29.
173. On the exercise of the reserve power *see,* Palmer, 27–33; R.Q. Quentin-Baxter, *The Governor-General's Constitutional Discretions: An Essay towards a Re-definition*, 10 VUWLR 289 (1980).

when no one party has a majority in the House to enable selection of a Prime Minister (in this circumstance the Governor-General would have the right to appoint a Prime Minister or initiate another election); (iv) to refuse to assent to a Bill which offends the basic tenets of the nation.

The reserve powers have not been exercised in recent times.

103. The Governor-General acts on the advice of responsible Ministers, and as a corollary has the right to information. Ministers are to give information to the Governor-General on any governmental matter which is requested.[174] This right was written into the Cabinet Office Manual and Ministers may ask officials to brief the Governor-General on specific matters.

174. Letters Patent constituting the Office of the Governor-General of New Zealand, cl. 16.

Chapter 3. The Legislature

§1. Organ of State

I. Brief History

104. With the signing of the Treaty of Waitangi by the Crown and Maori tribes of New Zealand in 1840, New Zealand became part of the British Empire. Thus, New Zealand came under the authority of the British monarchy and the Imperial Parliament at Westminster.

105. In 1852, the Imperial Parliament passed the New Zealand Constitution Act[175] 'to grant a Representative Constitution to the Colony of New Zealand'. This Act established representative government in New Zealand creating a General Assembly, consisting of the Governor, the Legislative Council and House of Representatives, and also for a network of Provincial Councils. History proved this structure to be ill-suited to the new colony.

106. The Legislative Council comprised members appointed for life. The House of Representatives was elected every five years by adult males who satisfied property-owning criteria.[176]

107. The 1852 Act established six provinces. Four more provinces followed. Each province was led by a Superintendent. The Superintendent and the Provincial Council were elected by the adult male population for a four-year term.[177]

The Governor had the power to veto provincial legislation.[178]

108. The Constitution Act did not set out in detail where the division of responsibilities between the provinces and central government would lie, but in practice the provincial governments dealt with what were then considered local government concerns: immigration, public works, waste lands, education, health, jails and police. As the population of New Zealand increased, so did the conflict between central and provincial government. The problem was solved in 1875 when the General Assembly abolished the provinces.[179]

109. From 1876 New Zealand had a centralized bicameral parliamentary system. The Legislative Council, the upper house, was to consist of ten or more members to be appointed by the Governor for life. The first two Maori members were appointed in 1872. Women became eligible for appointment in 1941 and the first two were appointed in 1946.

175. 15 and 16 Vict, Ch. 72.
176. Sections 7, 34, 40 and 42.
177. Sections 2, 3, 4, 7 and 13.
178. Section 29.
179. Abolition of the Provinces Act 1875.

110. The Leader of the Legislative Council (i.e., government spokesperson in that Chamber) was usually appointed to the Executive Council and also frequently held a ministerial portfolio in Cabinet. In most aspects its procedure was similar to that of the House of Representatives, the lower house.

The Legislative Council was active in its early years, and rejected several Bills passed by the House of Representatives. As a result, in 1891 government supporters were appointed to the Council and the term of office for councillors was changed from life to seven years. From then on the Legislative Council was effectively controlled by the government of the day, with successive governments making sure, if needed, that the Council contained a majority of their supporters.

In 1946, the National Party expressed the desire to either make the Council a more useful body or abolish it. In 1950, the Legislative Council membership was increased by twenty to ensure the passage of a government Bill to abolish it. The Bill was duly passed, and the New Zealand Legislative Council ceased to exist from 1 January 1951.[180]

II. Present Form

111. Parliament now consists of the Sovereign (or the Sovereign's representative, the Governor-General) and the House of Representatives.[181]

112. The House of Representatives is a body of members called Members of Parliament elected by the people. Under the Constitution Act 1986, the House is regarded as being continuously in existence, regardless of whether Parliament has expired or been dissolved. All Members of Parliament must be elected in accordance with the Electoral Act 1993.[182] Each Member of Parliament must take an oath of allegiance before he or she can take a seat or vote in the House.[183] The House elects its own Speaker at its first meeting after a general election. The person so elected as Speaker continues in office notwithstanding Parliament's expiration or dissolution, until the close of polling day at the next general election.[184]

The House of Representatives provides the forum for public debate and scrutiny of the action of the Executive in New Zealand.

III. The Franchise

113. The elected members of Parliament are chosen by the eligible voters in their constituency at general elections held every three years. These elections are based

180. Legislative Council Abolition Act 1950.
181. Constitution Act 1986, s. 14. The term Parliament officially replaced 'General Assembly' after the Constitution Act 1986 repealed the New Zealand Constitution Act 1852.
182. Constitution Act 1986, s. 10.
183. Section 11.
184. Sections 12 and 13.

on the democratic premise of one person one vote, with a virtually universal franchise. But this has not always been the case.

114. The New Zealand Constitution Act 1852 provided only a limited franchise: to a male land-holder or lease-holder over 21 years old, with a right to vote in each electorate where they held land (plural voting). This excluded women, poor or landless men, and most Maori (because of the tribal land tenure system).

In 1860, the right to vote was extended to miners who held miner's rights pursuant to the Miners Franchise Act 1860.

In 1867, four Maori seats were created in the House of Representatives by the Maori Representation Act. This was originally intended merely as a temporary provision, but it was made permanent nine years later by Parliament. Maori electors were restricted to all male adult Maori and half-castes. Thus Maori, although under-represented in proportion to their population, received universal male franchise before their European counterparts.

Eight years later the Lodgers Franchise Act 1875 extended the franchise to male ratepayers over 21 years of age.

The Qualification of Electors Act 1879 gave the vote to all British males over 21 years old who had lived in New Zealand for at least a year.

The next major extension in the franchise occurred in 1893, when women gained the right to vote (although they were not able to stand for Parliament until 1919). New Zealand was the first country in the world to grant votes to women. Plural voting was abolished in 1889 and the lease/landholding requirement replaced by a residential period in 1879.

115. Changes to the franchise since 1893 have been less significant. In 1924, it became compulsory for general electorate voters to register, and for Maori in 1956. Though this is legally enforceable by fines, the sanction has not been used. In 1927, postal or special voting was introduced. The voting age was lowered to twenty in 1969, then to eighteen in 1974.

116. Since 1975 British nationality is no longer a qualification for voting. Now all adult New Zealand citizens and permanent residents are qualified, provided that they meet the required residential requirements and are not subject to disqualification under the Act.[185]

117. New Zealand's present electoral system is provided for and governed by the Electoral Act 1993. The object of the Electoral Acts has been to provide the form and machinery of the electoral system, and to give special protection to essential elements of the system after abolition of the upper house.

185. Examples of disqualification are being detained under a Mental Health Act and having been found by a Court or a Judge to be unfit to stand trial, or serving a prison sentence of a term of three years or more. Electoral Act 1993, s. 80.

IV. Electoral Petitions

118. According to the Electoral Act 1993, the only way in which a person's election may be challenged is by petition.[186] Any elector or candidate (alleged or accepted) may present such a petition to the High Court, as long as the petition is presented within twenty-eight days from the declaration of election results.[187] Election petitions are heard before three judges of the High Court at the registry of the Court where the petition was filed.[188] The rules of evidence are waived slightly to enable the achievement of real justice, and to avoid focus on technicalities.[189] Once the Court has determined the legality of a person's election, it certifies its verdict in writing, and presents it to the Speaker of the House.[190] Where allegations of corrupt and illegal practices have been made in an election petition, the Court also reports to the Speaker on the findings on that issue.[191] If the allegations are found to be true, the Act provides that a report shall also be submitted to the Attorney-General.[192] There is no appeal from the decision of the High Court.[193]

§2. Legal Status of Legislature

I. Parliamentary Privileges and Immunities

119. New Zealand parliamentary privileges are derived from those of the United Kingdom Parliament[194] and New Zealand statute.

120. The privileges of the United Kingdom Parliament which the New Zealand Parliament now possesses evolved over several centuries. The freedom of debate in Parliament was recognized by Strodes Act 1512[195] and was confirmed in Article IX of the Bill of Rights 1688 which provides:[196] 'That the freedom of speech, and debates or proceedings in Parliament, ought not to be impeached or questioned in any Court or place outside Parliament.'

'Proceedings in Parliament' has been held to include Select Committees[197] and the control by the House of Representatives of its own internal affairs.[198]

121. Courts decline jurisdiction where parliamentary privilege is at issue; the matter is within Parliament's jurisdiction only. But, as the case of *Stockdale v.*

186. Section 229.
187. Sections 230 and 231.
188. Section 235.
189. Section 240.
190. Section 243.
191. Section 244.
192. Section 257.
193. Section 242.
194. Common Law.
195. 4 Hen 8, Ch. 8. Also known as the Privilege of Parliament Act 1512.
196. 1 Will and Mar, Sess 2, Ch. 2.
197. *Goffin v. Donnelly* (1881) 6 QBD 307.
198. *Bradlaugh v. Gosset* (1884) 12 QBD 271.

Hansard[199] showed, courts reserve the right to examine the claim of privilege to see whether it actually exists or not, as the law and custom of Parliament is part of the general law. An alteration of the law to create a privilege can only occur by statute. As a result of this case the Parliamentary Papers Act 1840 (UK) was passed which conferred absolute privilege on documents ordered by Parliament to be published.[200]

122. Members of Parliament have immunity from imprisonment under civil proceedings: *Goudy v. Duncombe.*[201] The reason for this is that the House has first call on its members; court proceedings (unless criminal) should not impede a member's duty to the House.

123. Parliament also has the right to punish those guilty of breach of privilege. The House can commit to prison any person on a general warrant, and no court may review this. It may also fine or order any other censure on the offending party. The power of Parliament to punish for contempt is equivalent to the power of a Royal court to punish any person who insulted or 'improperly' interfered with its proceedings. It was partially justified by the fact that the United Kingdom House of Commons was part of a court of law, the High Court of Parliament. It also served to ensure the Commons separation from the judiciary, because if the House of Commons could itself punish for contempt then it need not refer alleged cases of contempt to the courts, but could take its own action to protect its authority and dignity.

124. The New Zealand Constitution Act 1852 did not specify the privileges that the House of Representatives enjoyed. In 1854, a committee of the House of Representatives[202] was set up to inquire into privilege. It reported that the House had no inherent right or privilege but that it could claim privileges at common law incidental to its functions as a statutory body, in keeping with the 1841 Privy Council decision of *Keilly v. Carson.*[203] The Privileges Act 1856 was introduced but this did not go far enough. The power to punish contempt was the main privilege the House of Representatives lacked.

As a result the Parliamentary Privileges Act 1865 was passed. This gave the House the powers and privileges of the English House of Commons as at 1 January 1865. This rule is now incorporated in the Parliamentary Privilege Act 2014.[204] That Act was passed in response to a 2011 Supreme Court decision, *Attorney-General and Gow v. Leigh.*[205] The decision related to a defamation action brought against a Deputy Secretary of the Ministry for the Environment, who had briefed the Minister for the Environment in relation to a written question for oral answer in the

199. (1839) 9 A & E 1, 112 ER 1112.
200. In 1704, the House of Commons agreed that it had no power to create any privilege not already recognized by the known laws and customs of parliament. From then on privileges had to be created by legislation. New Zealand adheres to the same practice.
201. (1847) 1 Exch 430, 154 ER 183.
202. Votes and Proceedings of the House of Representatives 1854, Report No. 7.
203. (1842) 4 Moo PC 63; 13 ER 225.
204. Section 8.
205. [2011] NZSC 106, [2012] 2 NZLR 713.

House of Representatives. The Minister had used the information supplied to answer the parliamentary question. The respondent brought proceedings claiming the Deputy Secretary had defamed her in what he had told the Minister. The Deputy Secretary contended that the communication had taken place on an occasion of absolute privilege and that the claim should therefore be struck out. The Supreme Court, upholding the Court of Appeal, held the occasion on which the information was communicated with the Minister was one of qualified, rather than absolute, privilege.

Following the decision, the Privileges Committee produced a Report concluding that the Court's decision represented a significant shift in the interpretation of the scope of privilege.[206] It recommended legislation to restore privilege's scope to Parliament's previous understandings. It also made various other recommendations, including modernizing existing legislation and reaffirming certain other aspects of privilege. Those recommendations were accepted, and the Parliamentary Privilege Act 2014 was enacted. The Act does not comprehensively codify all aspects of parliamentary privilege.

There are two types of privilege (a) immunities of members, and (b) privilege in the nature of powers exercised collectively by the House.

125. Freedom of speech is enjoyed by Members of Parliament so long as it is deemed part of parliamentary proceedings; otherwise, no absolute privilege is enjoyed. 'Proceedings in Parliament' are defined expansively in section 10 of the Act, and include 'all words spoken and acts done in the course of, or for purposes of or incidental to, the transacting of the business of the House or of a committee'. The definition expressly excludes the use of a necessity test to determine whether words or acts are caught by the definition.

126. The Speaker may issue a certificate allowing an officer of Parliament or Member of Parliament from attendance in court as a witness or party in civil proceedings, or as a witness in a criminal proceeding. The Speaker must issue the certificate unless the Speaker thinks it may defeat the interests of justice or cause irreparable injury to a party to the proceeding. The certificate will expire at the end of the session during which the certificate was granted, or at the end of the calendar year after the calendar year during which the certificate was granted.[207] Members of Parliament are disqualified from jury service during their term.[208]

127. A range of other privileges are not legislated for, but section 8(1) of the Act states that the privileges, immunities and powers which were exercisable by the Commons House of Parliament of Great Britain and Ireland, its committees or its members as at 1 January 1865 are exercisable by the House, committees, and members as long as they are not inconsistent with, or repugnant to, the New Zealand

206. *Question of Privilege concerning the defamation action* Attorney-General and *Gow v. Leigh* (2013) AJHR I.17A.
207. Sections 26, 27, 28 and 30. Similar provisions exist in respect of the Speaker: s. 29.
208. Juries Act 1981, s. 8(b).

Constitution Act 1852. These privileges include the House's exclusive right to control its proceedings, and the House's power to discipline its members.

II. Standing Orders of the House of Representatives

128. The Standing Orders of the House of Representatives provide the code of conduct and procedure which govern the House of Representatives. The first Standing Orders came into effect in 1854.[209] The present orders are the Standing Orders 1996.[210]

III. Powers of the House of Representatives

129. The House of Representatives has power:

(a) To regulate its proceedings by Standing Orders having the force of law, free from interference by the courts. Parliament is self-regulating: 'The remedy for a Parliamentary wrong, if one has been committed, must be sought from Parliament, and cannot be gained from the courts.'[211]
(b) To determine the right to sit in the House (after the provisions of the Electoral Act have been complied with). This power has been exercised several times in New Zealand. If it is doubtful whether a person claiming to be a member is entitled to take a seat in the House, or that a member may have been disqualified from membership, the House can look into the matter, and, if necessary, order the Speaker to direct the Clerk of Writs to issue a new writ to fill the empty seat. This means that the House is interpreting the law as it applies to itself. It is allowed to do so as long as it does not act inconsistently with the Electoral Act 1993.
(c) To suspend or expel members (in addition to powers contained in the Electoral Act 1993). This is distinct from suspension for breach of order. The effects of suspension are set out in Standing Orders.[212] Such a member cannot enter the Chamber, vote or lodge questions or notices of motion. A suspended member may not serve on a Select Committee during the period of suspension. It is uncertain whether the House can expel a member. The Report of the Standing Orders Committee on the Law of Privilege and Related Matters on privilege[213] recommended that any power of the House to expel a member be abolished by legislation. No action has yet been taken on that report, so the position remains unclear.

---

209. *Parliamentary Debates* 1854–1855, 94.
210. Those Orders have been amended several times: in August 1996, September 1999, December 2003, August 2005, September 2008, October 2011 and July 2014.
211. *British Railways Board v. Pickin* [1974] AC 765 per Lord Wilberforce at 793. *See also, Naomi Shire Council v. Attorney-General (New South Wales)* [1980] 2 NSWLR 639.
212. Standing Order 95.
213. 1987–1990 AJHR I.18B, para. 31.

(d) To arrest (by Speaker's warrant) persons guilty of contempt or breach of privilege. The New Zealand Parliament acquired this power by the Colonial Laws Validity Act 1865 (UK). In theory the rules of natural justice do not apply to or bind Parliament, and no court can review its decisions. This power has not yet been exercised in New Zealand.

(e) To fine, reprimand or exclude from the precincts (of Parliament buildings) for contempt or breach of privilege.[214] The New Zealand Parliament has exercised the power to fine three times, in 1896, 1901 and 1903. It is doubtful now whether the House would fine without legislation to back it up. In the Report of the Standing Orders Committee on the Law of Privilege and Related Matters[215] it was recommended that Parliament should enact legislation providing it with power to fine for contempt. This suggests that Parliament does not enjoy that power at present, but the situation is not clear-cut.
The Crown, as legal owner, permits the House of Representatives to exercise control over Parliament buildings and grounds while it is in session. The House delegates this control to the Speaker, but any action taken under this power is usually by a resolution of the House.[216]

(f) To administer oaths to witnesses. This power is contained in the Parliamentary Privilege Act 2014:[217]

> The House or a committee respectively may, for the purpose of taking evidence on oath or affirmation from a witness examined before the House or that committee, administer an oath or affirmation to the witness.

IV. Procedure for Raising Privilege

130. The procedure for raising a matter of privilege in the House is prescribed by Standing Orders.[218] At the commencement of each Parliament a Select Committee is set up to deal with matters of privilege. A member who wishes to raise a matter of privilege must refer the matter, in writing, to the Speaker, who determines whether a question of privilege is involved. A matter must be important to be raised as a question of privilege. The Speaker will not entertain trivial matters. An allegation of breach of privilege must be formulated precisely, thereby giving the person against whom it was made an opportunity to respond.

---

214. A case involving exclusion from the precincts involved a courier who refused to answer questions before the Parliamentary Privileges Committee. The courier and associated companies were banned from the precincts. *See, Parliamentary Debates* 1992, vol. 528, 10626–10631.
215. 1987–1990 AJHR I.18B, para. 30.
216. Parliament grounds are open to the public and may be used to stage meetings and rallies. However, there are conditions on the use of the grounds. For example, participants must assemble and disperse in an orderly fashion and are not permitted to breach the peace. *See, Melser v. Police* [1967] NZLR 437.
217. Section 24.
218. Standing Orders 401–408.

131. Where the matter in question involves another member of the House, notification must be given to that member by the member raising the privilege question. The Speaker also must notify any other member involved that the matter is to be reported to the House.

After the Speaker has decided that a matter does involve a question of privilege and has reported it to the House, the matter is referred to the Privileges Committee for consideration.

V. Contempt

132. The House in New Zealand tends to punish a breach of privilege by treating the breach as a contempt, and then punishing the contempt. But the term also includes any interference with the proper performance of any aspect of the House or its functions.

If there is precedent, or if an action can reasonably be regarded as contempt even if there is no precedent, then the House will discipline that action.

Examples of contempt include disobedience to the orders of committees, disobedience to the rules or orders of the House, acceptance of fees for professional services connected with proceedings in Parliament, and a member's absence from the House without leave.[219]

VI. Members' Pecuniary Interests

133. Under the Standing Orders a member must declare any pecuniary interests which the member has in any business of the House, before participating in any consideration of the business.[220] Financial interest is defined in the Standing Orders. It encompasses a financial benefit which a member may gain either personally or through a trust, company or other business entity in which the member holds an appreciable interest, and as a result of the House's consideration of the matter. A financial interest can extend to an interest held by a member's spouse or dependent child.[221] In the event of a dispute the Speaker will decide whether a member holds a financial interest.[222] The aim of these rules is to stop members from furthering their business interests during their term as representatives of the people in their electorate. In practice, most members find it best to state any personal interest they have in the result of any issue being discussed, in anticipation of possible charges of impropriety. Furthermore, all members are required to disclose certain assets and interests in an annual Register of Pecuniary Interests of Members of Parliament. This is designed to promote transparency and accountability, and the requirements are set out in appendix B of the Standing Orders of the House of Representatives.

219. Standing Orders 409–410.
220. Standing Order 165.
221. Standing Order 164.
222. Standing Order 166.

134. Additional requirements apply to Ministers' interests. Ministers are responsible for ensuring no conflict exists or appears to exist between their personal interests and their public duty. Since 2012, the Department of Prime Minister and Cabinet releases information annually about the management of ministerial conflicts of interests, which includes information on the matter at issue and the action taken to manage the conflict.

VII. Sessions

135. While Parliament is in session, Members of Parliament are required to attend all sittings: Tuesday and Wednesday 2 p.m. to 6 p.m. and 7.30 p.m. to 10 p.m.; Thursday 2 p.m. to 6 p.m.[223] If urgency or extraordinary urgency is taken on a matter the sittings times are extended accordingly to proceed with the matter to a completion.[224] Since 1984 Parliament has sat regularly.

A motion for the adjournment of the House can only be moved by a Minister.[225] The Speaker has the power to adjourn the House or suspend a sitting.[226]

VIII. Prorogation, Dissolution and Expiration

136. The Governor-General may, by proclamation, summon, prorogue or dissolve Parliament.[227] The House's sittings are broken into sessions by the Governor-General's proroguing Parliament. A session lasts from the time when the Governor-General summons Parliament till it is prorogued. Prorogation brings its sittings to a halt until the next session of Parliament.

Once prorogued, the House cannot meet until the Governor-General again summons it. Any business the House is dealing with does not lapse on prorogation and may be resumed in the next session of that Parliament. However, any parliamentary business lapses on the dissolution or expiration of that Parliament, but may be reinstated in a session of the next Parliament.[228]

137. Prorogation and dissolution differ in that the latter not only brings the session to an end, but also ends that Parliament and the term of office of its members, and provokes a general election. Usually Parliament is prorogued just before being dissolved. The Speaker continues in office notwithstanding the dissolution or expiration of Parliament until the close of polling day of the next general election.[229]

138. Each term of Parliament is restricted to three years from the day fixed for the return of the writs issued for the last preceding general election, and no

223. Standing Order 45.
224. Standing Orders 57–61.
225. Standing Order 49.
226. Standing Order 50.
227. Constitutional Act 1986, s. 18.
228. Constitutional Act 1986, s. 20.
229. Constitutional Act 1986, s. 13.

longer.[230] Unless Parliament is sooner dissolved, it expires on that date, and the Governor-General will order a general election.

The prorogation, dissolution or expiration of Parliament has no legal effect on the House of Representatives, which, under section 10 of the Constitution Act 1986, is regarded as always in existence. The latest date on which a new Parliament is required to meet is six weeks after the day fixed for the return of the writs for the election of the members of the House of Representatives.[231]

§3. Competence of the New Zealand Legislature

139. By the Statute of Westminster Adoption Act 1947, New Zealand adopted the Statute of Westminster 1931. At this point New Zealand gained a supreme law-making competence.

140. Before 1947, the competence of Parliament was restricted. The New Zealand Parliament derived its original law-making powers from statute enacted by the United Kingdom Parliament.

The New Zealand Constitution Act 1852 granted the colony responsible self-government. The General Assembly was empowered by section 53: 'to make laws for the peace, order, and good government of New Zealand, provided that no such laws be repugnant to the law of England'.

This law-making power was therefore not supreme. It was subject to several limitations which were successively eroded over the years:[232]

(1) *Repugnancy*: Legislation could not be passed which was repugnant to the laws of England.[233]
(2) *Extra-territoriality*: The 1852 Act was silent on the power of New Zealand to legislate extraterritorially and the issue was the subject of some litigation.[234]
(3) *Entrenched provisions of the Constitution*: Up until 1857, the New Zealand Parliament had power to amend only specified provisions of the 1852 Constitution Act. In 1857[235] power was given to amend all but twenty-one sections of the Act.[236] In 1862, power was given to alter a further section.[237] After the provinces were abolished, five further sections became inoperative. This left fifteen sections unable to be altered such as section 32 establishing the General Assembly and section 53 (the law-making power) itself. In 1947, pursuant to the New

230. Constitutional Act 1986, s. 17. This provision is entrenched by s. 268 of the Electoral Act 1993.
231. Constitutional Act 1986, s. 19.
232. For a full discussion of this evolution, *see*, J.L. Robson, *New Zealand: The Development of Its Laws and Constitution*, 54–64 (2d ed., Stevens and Sons 1967).
233. Colonial Laws Validity Act 1865 (UK), ss 2, 3 and 4. On the adoption of the Statute of Westminster 1931 repugnancy was no longer operative: s. 2.
234. For example, *see, The Queen v. Fineberg* [1968] NZLR 119. Power to legislate extraterritorially was expressly provided for in the Statute of Westminster 1931.
235. New Zealand Constitution Amendment Act 1857 (UK) 20 and 21 Vict, Ch. 53.
236. Section 2.
237. 25 and 26 Vict, Ch. 48.

Zealand Constitution Amendment (Request and Consent) Act 1947 requesting imperial entrenchment, the New Zealand Constitution (Amendment) Act 1947 (UK) eventually gave the Assembly full power to amend the New Zealand Constitution Act 1852.[238]

(4) *Reservation:* Under the 1852 Act, power was given to the Governor, at his or her discretion to decline to assent to a duly passed Bill, or to reserve it for the Royal pleasure.[239] In certain cases reservation was obligatory. For example, alterations to the salary of the Governor-General.[240] These provisions were eroded over the years.[241]

(5) *Disallowance:* The 1852 Act required the Governor to transmit to the Secretary of State a copy of Acts which he or she had assented to. The Crown was permitted two years to disallow any Act.[242]

141. The supremacy of the law-making power of the New Zealand Parliament is reflected in the New Zealand Constitution Act 1986, which reads:[243]

(1) The Parliament of New Zealand continues to have full power to make laws.
(2) No Act of the Parliament of the United Kingdom passed after the commencement of this Act shall extend to New Zealand as part of its law.

Parliament is the highest law-making authority in New Zealand.

142. The Bill of Rights 1688, an inherited statute, protects Parliament's authority. Article I of the Bill states 'That the pretended power of suspending of laws, or the execution of laws, by regal authority, without consent of Parliament, is illegal.' This provision was the basis of the High Court decision in *Fitzgerald v. Muldoon.*[244] The Prime Minister had made statements in the press which purported to suspend the operation of the New Zealand Superannuation Act 1974. Such statements were found to be illegal. It was held that Parliament was sovereign and had a right to legislate which could not be overridden by any person or body.[245] The Prime Minister's announcement in the course of his official duties was made by regal authority within the meaning of that expression in Article I of the Bill of Rights 1688.[246]

238. Section 1.
239. Section 56.
240. Section 65.
241. The New Zealand Constitution Amendment Act 1973 removed the final elements of colonial status.
242. Section 58. Finally repealed by the New Zealand Constitution Amendment Act 1973.
243. Section 15.
244. [1976] 2 NZLR 615.
245. Page 622.
246. The end result of the matter was that Parliament passed legislation, giving legal effect to the Prime Minister's statements. Superannuation Schemes Act 1976, ss 3 and 10.

I. Broadcasting of Parliamentary Debates

143. Parliamentary proceedings have been broadcast by radio since 1936.[247] Standing Orders require that the proceedings of the House shall be broadcast on radio during all sitting hours. It also provides that the House proceedings be available for television coverage. Televised proceedings must comply with the rules as set out in Appendix D of the Standing Orders.[248]

II. Types of Bills

144. There are four types of Bills which can come before the House. They are: Government Bills, Local Bills, Members' Bills and Private Bills.[249]

All Bills must contain the appropriate enacting formula.[250] In addition, a private Bill must contain a statement declaring it to be a private Act, and include a preamble which specifies the reasons why the legislation is necessary.[251]

In general Bills must relate to one subject matter area only. However, there are specific provisions for omnibus Bills.[252]

Standing Orders also provide that the Attorney-General must highlight any parts of a Bill that appear to be inconsistent with the New Zealand Bill of Rights Act 1990.[253]

Bills must be read three times before they can be passed by the House.[254] Special provisions apply to proposals for entrenchment.[255]

145. There are also special rules for particular types of Bills. For example, Appropriation and Imprest Supply Bills are subject to special requirements.[256]

III. General Process

146. The following details the stages in the passage of a Bill:

INTRODUCTION
↓
FIRST READING
↓
SELECT COMMITTEE CONSIDERATION

247. Now live debates in the House are broadcast in a Parliament TV channel, and readings of Bills are available online at www.inthehouse.co.nz.
248. Standing Order 46.
249. Standing Order 253.
250. Standing Order 254.
251. Standing Order 258.
252. Standing Orders 262–263.
253. Standing Order 265. This is also required by s. 7 of the New Zealand Bill of Rights Act 1990.
254. Standing Order 268.
255. Standing Order 266.
256. Standing Order 270 and Chapter 6.

↓
SECOND READING
↓
COMMITTEE OF THE WHOLE HOUSE
↓
THIRD READING
↓
ROYAL ASSENT

A. Introduction and First Reading

147. Chapter 5 of the Standing Orders deals with the procedure for various stages of a Bill. Government bills are introduced by the Leader of the House informing the Clerk that it is the Government's intention to introduce a Bill. Copies of the Bill must be available for circulation to members. At the next sitting of the House following notice, the Clerk announces the Bill's introduction as an item of general business, and it is set down for a first reading on the third sitting day following its introduction. To begin the first reading debate, the Minister in charge of the Bill will move that the Bill be read for a first time, and speaks to the motion. A debate follows that motion, which is limited to twelve speeches of 10 minutes. At the end of the debate the Speaker puts the question if the Bill will be read the first time. If it is, it will be referred to a select committee (which committee it is referred to is proposed by the Minister). A slightly different process applies for Members' and Local and Private Bills.

B. Select Committees

148. The easiest way for a member of the public to have a direct impact on the legislative process is through the Select Committee system.

The role of Select Committees was much increased in 1985 when the Standing Orders were revised. Chapter 4 of the Orders deals with the formation and administration of committees. Some thirteen subject committees are set up,[257] but the House may establish other committees.

The Business Committee determines the size of each Committee and the overall membership of select Committees must be proportional to party membership in the House.[258] Usually they are chaired by a government member.

149. All Bills except Money Bills and Bills under urgency are referred to a Select Committee dealing with that subject area after the Bill's first reading. The Select Committee is required to report on the Bill and propose amendments to it. Petitions presented by the public are also given to Select Committees for report, as

257. Standing Order 188.
258. Standing Order 185.

are the expenditure estimates of relevant/associated departments. A Select Committee cannot consider a Bill that has not been referred to it.[259]

150. A Select Committee report must be presented to the House and debated.[260]

151. Select Committees usually ask for submissions from the public. Committees have the power 'to send for persons, papers and records'[261] to assist in their investigations. Under Standing Orders[262] they may meet anywhere in New Zealand, which assists their ability to gather evidence. Submissions are made by large numbers of people with an interest in the area of consideration – whether individual or interest groups and associations. Although a Select Committee usually sits in public,[263] provision exists for evidence to be heard in private, if that is felt to be desirable. Submissions may be delivered either in writing or orally: most are made in writing in the interests of simplicity. Submissions are not guaranteed a reading and they may be refused if they are late, irrelevant or offensive.

152. The impact of public submissions to Select Committees is difficult to gauge. Undoubtedly the impact varies according to the prestige and standing within the relevant subject area of the person or group making the submission. All people and organizations who make representations to a Select Committee are listed in an appendix to the committee's report. Sometimes submissions are referred to in the report, whether generally or by name. It is possible to argue, however, that by the time a Bill has reached the Select Committee stage, it is too late for it to be altered substantially. The best chance of being influential is to work with departmental officials and Ministers early in policy formation.

153. Select Committees are appointed by the House, and derive their powers from that appointment. Much of their business comes from the House and they are answerable to it. The specific, permanent committees set up by the Standing Orders of the House include:

(i) The Regulations Review Committee.[264] This committee reviews all regulations and reports on them and proposed regulations. People aggrieved by the operation of any regulation may complain to the committee about this. The Committee is given various grounds for the referral to the House of regulations about which it is concerned.[265]

(ii) The Privileges Committee,[266] which considers matters relating to or concerning parliamentary privilege.

259. Standing Order 189(3).
260. Standing Orders 295–300.
261. Standing Order 196.
262. Standing Order 192.
263. Standing Order 222.
264. Standing Orders 184 and 318.
265. Standing Orders 319 and 320.
266. Standing Orders 184 and 401.

(iii) Thirteen 'subject' committees,[267] in the fields of:
- commerce;
- education and science;
- finance and expenditure;
- foreign affairs, defence and trade;
- government administration;
- health;
- justice and electoral;
- law and order;
- local government and environment;
- Maori affairs;
- primary production;
- social services;
- transport and industrial relations.

(iv) The Officers of Parliament Committee, which considers and recommends to the House: an estimate of appropriations for each Office of Parliament, an auditor for each Office of Parliament, proposals for the creating of an Officer of Parliament, and the appointments of persons as Officers of Parliament.[268]

(v) The Standing Orders Committee which reviews, considers and reports on matters relating to the Standing Orders, procedures and practices of the House.[269]

154. There is also a non-parliamentary Legislation Advisory Committee, appointed by the Minister of Justice. It comprises a variety of people such as representatives from the Ministry of Justice and Crown Law Office, academics and practitioners. It sets standards for good legislation by settling Guidelines on Process and Content of Legislation, and reviews Government Bills introduced into Parliament against those Guidelines.[270] If a Bill is inconsistent with the Guidelines, the Committee may make a submission to the relevant Select Committee.

155. In addition, the Attorney-General, under the New Zealand Bill of Rights Act 1990,[271] is responsible for bringing to the attention of the House of Representatives any provision of a Bill introduced into the House which appears to be inconsistent with that Act.

C. Second Reading

156. This is the stage at which the House is asked to adopt, in principle, the Bill before it. At this point there is the major debate on the proposal, which is much wider than that allowed at any other stage, though matters raised must still be relevant to the Bill.

267. Standing Order 188.
268. Standing Orders 184 and 395.
269. Standing Orders 7 and 180.
270. Particularly those with public law ramifications.
271. Section 7.

D. *Consideration by the Committee of the Whole House*

157. This is where detailed clause by clause consideration of the Bill by the House takes place. This stage gives all members an opportunity to participate in a thorough scrutiny of the Bill, and to move amendments. Each time the House goes into committee, the Speaker leaves the Chair without putting any question. The Deputy Speaker or, in the Deputy Speaker's absence, the Assistant Speaker, acts as Chairman for the committee's duration.[272]

158. The committee has power to make amendments to Bills referred to it, provided the amendments are relevant to the subject matter of the Bill.

There are several types of amendments which are inadmissible. These include:

- Amendments involving an appropriation of public money, unless earlier recommended to the House by a message from the Governor-General.
- Amendments inconsistent with a previous decision of that committee. An amendment which has been lost on one clause cannot be proposed again on another.
- Amendments proposing an increase in taxation.
- Amendments to omit a clause.

159. Once the Bill has been fully considered, the Chairperson reports it, with amendments made, to the House.[273] The Chairperson puts a motion that the report be adopted; this is decided without amendment or debate.[274]

E. *Third Reading*

160. The motion is moved for the third reading. Sometimes this is followed by a debate. Any debate that occurs is constrained. Members must restrict themselves to the general principles of the Bill as it has emerged from the Committee of the Whole House. One of the principal uses of this debate is to record (in *Hansard*) arguments advanced during the Committee stage. The third reading debate is in the nature of a summing-up.

When the motion on the third reading has been put and agreed to, the Bill is taken to have passed through the House of Representatives.

F. *Royal Assent*

161. The Constitution Act 1986 reads:[275] 'A Bill passed by the House of Representatives shall become law when the Sovereign or the Governor-General assents to it and signs it in token of such assent.'

---

272. Standing Orders 170–172.
273. Standing Order 182.
274. Standing Order 183.
275. Chapter V of the Standing Orders deals with the passage of a Bill through all stages, including assent.

The Governor-General does not, by convention, refuse assent but the Bill could be returned to the House with proposed amendments if for example there is a mistake in the form of the Bill.[276]

IV. Hansard (New Zealand Parliamentary Debates)

162. This is the verbatim transcript and official record of all debates and speeches made in the House of Representatives. It includes also questions and answers, but not debates when the House is in Committee.

V. Parliamentary Questions

163. Each day the House sits, it deals with oral questions lodged.[277] Twelve oral questions to Ministers may be accepted each day.[278] Following questions to Ministers, urgent questions and question to other members may also be asked.[279] Questions can serve several purposes. First there are the 'Dorothy Dix' questions, those asked of a Minister by a member of the same party, which allows the Minister and the Government to appear in a favourable light.

164. Members often ask a series of questions for the purpose of gathering information on a particular topic or policy, which can be used later in other debates, or to supply pressure groups or constituents with information. The main purpose of questions is to maintain the accountability of the Executive to the public. It is the role of the Opposition to expose the shortcomings of the Government. Ministers are required to answer; they cannot refuse. A Minister can be questioned on any matter relating to public affairs with which that Minister is officially connected, about proceedings in the House, or any matter of administration for which the Minister is responsible.[280] This gives a very wide scope for questions which can be asked relating to ministerial responsibility, but questions about a Minister acting in his or her personal capacity are out of order. They must relate to the Minister's portfolio. No questions are asked without previous notice of the question having been received by the person who is to answer it.

VI. Budget and Finances

165. Parliament is the provider of the money for the Executive to operate. Without the necessary approval of Parliament for revenue gathering and expenditure,

276. For a commentary on problems with the New Zealand legislative process *see,* G. Palmer, *Unbridled Power: An Interpretation of New Zealand's Constitution and Government*, 139–161 (2d ed., Oxford U. Press 1987).
277. Standing Order 383.
278. Standing Order 381.
279. Standing Orders 379 and 388.
280. Standing Order 378.

government will cease to function, as the Executive cannot itself make appropriations. The Constitution Act states:[281]

> It shall not be lawful for the Crown, except by or under an Act of Parliament, –
>
> (a) to levy a tax; or
> (b) to borrow money or to receive any money borrowed from any person; or
> (c) to spend any public money.

This was provided originally in the Bill of Rights 1688.[282] The financial legislation is probably of more constitutional significance than most other business of the House, because it is the Crown's need for supply which ensures that Parliament meets at least once by 30 June of each year.

166. The Crown's recommendation that a money Bill proceed has two elements. The first is the authority for the issue of public money. The second is the use of that money for a particular purpose. Each item of expenditure requires a separate vote in the annual Appropriation Act and Imprest Supply Acts; no expenditure can be made unless as expressly authorized by an appropriation or other authority by or under an Act.[283] The Public Finance Act 1989 also states that the authority to expend cash or incur costs provided by an appropriation under an Appropriation Act lapses at the end of each financial year to which the Act relates, or at the end of the period specified in the Appropriation Act, as long as it is not more than five years.[284] The main appropriation Bill for each financial year must be introduced in the House before the end of the first month of each financial year, unless the House resolves otherwise.[285]

167. Each vote in the Appropriation Bill is subject to scrutiny, first by the Finance and Expenditure Committee and then by the Committee of the Whole House.[286]

168. Emergency expenditure of money or costs can also occur where there is a national state of emergency or state of civil defence, or any situation which affects the public health or safety of New Zealand.[287]

281. Section 22.
282. Article IV.
283. Public Finance Act 1989, s. 4. Not all appropriation has to be made in the annual Appropriation Act. Some appropriation is made in other acts. For example, the salaries of judges is appropriated by s. 9A of the Judicature Act 1908, which reads: 'There shall be paid to the Chief Justice, to the other Judges of the Supreme Court, to the President of the Court of Appeal, to the other Judges of the Court of Appeal, and to the other Judges, out of public money, without further appropriation than this section [salaries as determined by the Remuneration Authority].'
284. Public Finance Act 1989, s. 10.
285. Public Finance Act 1989, s. 12.
286. Standing Orders 337–340.
287. Public Finance Act, s. 25.

169. Money is issued from the Crown Bank Accounts and Departmental Accounts. These accounts hold all public money, and all government expenditure or costs are charged against them.

170. The Controller and Auditor-General is established under the Public Audit Act 2001. The Auditor-General is an officer of Parliament who is appointed by the Governor-General on the recommendation of the House of Representatives.[288] The Auditor-General is also a corporation sole.[289] It is the auditor of every public entity.[290] It answers to no Minister, only to Parliament itself. The Office has access to all Government accounts and contracts.

If the Auditor-General has reason to believe that any money to be paid into a Departmental Bank Account may be used illegally or inconsistently with the purpose for which it was appropriated, a part or the whole of the statement may be refused, so that payment cannot go ahead.[291]

171. The Public Finance Act 1989 provides for various principles of fiscal responsibility. These factors include reducing Crown debt to, and maintaining it at, prudent levels.[292] It also provides for a budget policy statement to be published by 31 March in each year. That statement must specify the Government's overarching policy goals and the policy areas which the Government will focus on in that year and its budgetary intentions for the financial year.[293] The Minister of Finance is required to table a fiscal strategy report stating the Government's long-term objectives and short-term intentions for fiscal policy, assessing the consistency of the economic and fiscal update with the short-term intentions and giving projections for the following ten years.[294] Economic updates must be published[295] including prior to a general election.[296] Economic statements made under the Act must include reference to all Government decisions that may affect the fiscal forecast, and must be accompanied by statements of responsibility for the fiscal statement.[297]

VII. Delegated Legislation

172. Parliament does not enact all law in New Zealand. Because of the pressure on parliamentary time and the detail which some law requires, Parliament delegates authority to make some legislation; for example, to individual Ministers and to local

288. Public Audit Act 2001, s. 7.
289. Public Audit Act 2001, s. 10.
290. Public Audit Act 2001, s. 14.
291. Public Finance Act 1989, s. 65ZA.
292. Section 26G.
293. Section 26M.
294. Section 26I–26L.
295. Section 26S.
296. Section 26T.
297. Section 26N.

government bodies. Law enacted by delegated authority is called delegated legislation or subordinate or subsidiary legislation. The most common form is regulations made by the Governor-General in Council.

173. The amount of subsidiary legislation made each year is far greater than the amount of legislation made by Parliament. There are no prescribed procedures for making regulations, such as public debate before promulgation, although consultation may be required by the enabling statute. Failure to comply with the enabling statute invalidates the regulation.

174. In 1962, the Delegated Legislation Committee studied the issue.[298] In its report it recommended that a standard form of enabling provision be adopted so that the precise limits of the law-making power being delegated could be set down as clearly as possible, that the Court's jurisdiction to review regulations should not be reduced in such provisions, and that the Statutes Revision Committee have the power to review regulations referred to it. All these recommendations were implemented.

175. Regulations must be made pursuant to a statute. If there is no enabling provision in the statute it is purported to have been made under, or the regulation exceeds the authority provided, it is ultra vires.

176. Regulations are not made by Parliament and are therefore not excluded from judicial review. The Supreme Court decision of *Reade v. Smith*[299] stated that a regulation is open to judicial review if there is a question of fact or law involved in the decision-making, and that if the regulation is inconsistent with the objects and provisions of the enabling statute it will be declared ultra vires.

177. In 1985, Parliament established a Regulations Review Committee.[300] All regulations are automatically referred to the Committee for investigation. In addition, a Minister can refer draft regulations to the Committee, the Committee can examine any regulation-making power in a Bill under consideration by another Select Committee, and the Committee can bring any other matter relating to regulations to the attention of the House.

The grounds upon which the Committee can draw the House's special attention to a regulation are where it:[301]

(a) is not in accordance with the general objects and intentions of the statute under which it is made;
(b) trespasses unduly on personal rights and liberties;
(c) appears to make some unusual or unexpected use of the powers conferred by the enactment under which it is made;

298. Report of the Committee on Delegated Legislation 1962 AJHR I.18.
299. [1959] NZLR 996.
300. *See,* now Standing Orders 318–325.
301. Standing Order 319.

(d) unduly makes the rights and liberties of persons dependent upon administrative decisions which are not subject to review on their merits by a judicial or other independent tribunal;
(e) excludes the jurisdiction of the courts without explicit authorization in the enactment under which it is made;
(f) contains matter more appropriate for parliamentary enactment;
(g) is retrospective where this is not expressly authorized by the enactment under which it is made;
(h) was not made in compliance with particular notice and consultation procedures prescribed by applicable enactments;
(i) for any other reason concerning its form or purport, calls for elucidation.

The Committee may also act on complaints received from the public. A unanimous resolution of the Committee is required to decline investigation of such a complaint.[302]

178. Legislation has also been enacted to ensure Parliament keeps a tighter control on delegated legislation. The Legislation Act 2012 requires all regulations (which are part of a broader category of instruments referred to in the Act as legislative instruments) to be laid before the House and published.

It is also now compulsory that, on the making of a new legislative instrument, a notice be published in the *New Zealand Gazette* with the legislative instrument's title, date, enabling statute, its number and the place where it can be purchased.[303]

179. Under the Legislation Act 2012 the House is able to disallow regulations. Disallowance takes place on the passing of the resolution or on a date specified in the resolution.[304] A disallowance has the effect of revoking the regulation,[305] and will revive any Act or regulation which the disallowed regulation has purported to amend or repeal or revoke.[306]

There is also provision for automatic disallowance in some cases. This occurs where a Member of Parliament who is also a member of the Regulations Review Committee gives notice to disallow a regulation. If it is not earlier dealt with by the House, the regulation will be automatically disallowed after twenty-one days. This does not include time in which Parliament is not sitting.[307]

VIII. Parliamentary Counsel Office

180. This office was established under the Statutes Drafting and Compilation Act 1920,[308] and continued under the Legislation Act 2012.[309] It is an Office of

302. Standing Order 320.
303. Legislation Act 2012, s. 12.
304. Section 42.
305. Section 44.
306. Section 45.
307. Section 43.
308. Section 2.
309. Section 58.

Parliament with a monopoly of government legislation drafting except that, pursuant to the Legislation Act 2012, the Governor-General may by Order in Council instruct the Inland Revenue Department to draft Bills.[310] The office is under the control of the Attorney-General.[311]

The office of the Chief Parliamentary Counsel was also established under the Statutes Drafting and Compilation Act 1920[312] and continued under the Legislation Act 2012.[313]

310. Sections 59 and 60.
311. Section 58.
312. Section 6.
313. Section 34.

Chapter 4. The Executive

181. The executive arm of the New Zealand Government is formally constituted by the Letters Patent Constituting the Office of Governor-General of New Zealand.[314] Those Letters establish the Executive Council, the purpose of which is to advise the Sovereign and the Governor-General in the government of New Zealand.[315] The Executive Council is to be made up of persons appointed to the Executive Council from among members of Parliament in New Zealand.[316]

Membership of the Executive Council is not, however, limited to or synonymous with Cabinet. Ministers outside Cabinet may attend. The meetings of the Council are chaired by the Governor-General (although the Governor-General is not a member) or in the Governor-General's absence, by the most senior Minister present. Regardless of who chairs the meeting, there must be at least two of other Ministers present throughout.[317]

§1. Cabinet

182. Primarily, executive power in New Zealand government resides in the Cabinet. There is, however, no formal law relating to the Cabinet in the New Zealand Constitution, and the method for selection of members of Cabinet and the role of Cabinet varies according to the party in power. In a National Government, the Prime Minister chooses the Ministers and the portfolio responsibilities.

183. The Cabinet usually contains about twenty Ministers and the Attorney-General. In addition there may be Ministers outside Cabinet, and Parliamentary Under-Secretaries. All these positions are held under warrant given by the Governor-General.[318] The actual structure and role of Cabinet is nowhere defined. It is a creature of constitutional convention, inherited from the Westminster system. Therefore, the nature of Cabinet changes with each administration.

Cabinet is always the dominant actor in New Zealand politics. It is in Cabinet that decisions are made on Government spending, policy and the content of legislation. Cabinet coordinates the administration of the public service and it also acts to ensure the political survival of its Government.

314. SR 1983/225 as amended by SR 1987/8, and SR 2006/219.
315. Clause VII.
316. Clause VIII.
317. Clause IX. The Council had an important role as the advisory body to the Governor in colonial times. Cabinet has usurped the Council's policy-making functions. Now, the Council meets briefly each week to perform clearly defined functions and tender advice to the Governor-General. This includes the promulgation of subsidiary legislation, the exercise of the prerogative of mercy, and the establishment of Royal Commissions. Meetings are usually brief, because the decisions have already been confirmed in Cabinet.
318. For a full discussion of Cabinet see, G. Palmer, *Unbridled Power: An Interpretation of New Zealand's Constitution and Government* 34–63 (2d ed., Oxford U. Press 1987).

184. It is impossible for all Cabinet business to be determined in the weekly Cabinet meetings. This led to the rise of a Cabinet committee system. Matters are thoroughly researched and policy initiatives determined in Cabinet committees. This improves the efficiency of Cabinet. The number and type of committees depends on the individual Cabinet.

Cabinet committees allow Ministers to hear submissions from public servants. They also allow discussion in detail, something which does not occur in Cabinet because of the length of Cabinet agendas.

185. At Cabinet meetings, each item on the agenda is discussed briefly until agreement is reached. If there is no agreement, the matter will be deferred, or the recommendation changed. No votes are taken. Meetings are confidential and private. However, the minutes of decisions taken at Cabinet meetings (by the Cabinet Secretary) become the source of authority for Government action at all levels. Cabinet papers are all subject to the usual rules about the release of official information under the Official Information Act 1982, and so may be released if a request is made for them. Some information in Cabinet papers may be withheld from disclosure for the reasons listed under that Act (e.g., because releasing it would prejudice national security or seriously damage the economy of New Zealand).

186. It is the convention in the New Zealand system that collective responsibility prevails in Cabinet. This means that all Ministers take responsibility for Cabinet action. Personal feelings are irrelevant. If a Minister wishes to criticize a Cabinet decision publicly, he or she must first resign or expect to be asked to resign. The extent to which the doctrine is enforced depends on the issue at stake and the style of leadership. To avoid divisiveness in Government, the Prime Minister may well require an outspoken Minister's resignation.

Individual ministerial responsibility is also an important notion. In principle, Ministers are responsible for the actions of their departments, even when the fault does not lie with the Minister. However, this notion has limits. Even though Ministers bear the brunt of criticism for departmental action, they are not usually expected to resign unless there has been some personal impropriety by the Minister.

187. In other respects, Ministers have the same privileges and responsibilities as ordinary parliamentary members. This includes the right to freedom of speech within the House of Representatives, free air travel and allowances for travel within New Zealand. They also have the same responsibilities as ordinary backbench Members of Parliament to their constituencies.

§2. REMUNERATION

188. The Members of Parliament (Remuneration and Services) Act 2013 provides for the salaries and allowances of members of Parliament.[319] The salaries and

319. Members of Parliament (Remuneration and Services) Act 2013, s. 8.

allowances are fixed by the Remuneration Authority.[320] Money required to fund these salaries and any allowances are a permanent charge on public money without further appropriation.[321]

189. There is no specific superannuation scheme for members; however, recognition is given to members who choose to join a superannuation scheme[322] by way of the payment of a subsidy in respect of the member. The subsidy is determined by the Remuneration Authority.[323]

§3. THE PRIME MINISTER

190. Theoretically, the Prime Minister is no different from any other Minister in Cabinet; however, the traditional notion that the Prime Minister is *primus inter pares* has slowly been eroded.

191. In both the National and Labour Parties, the Party leader and deputy leader, upon becoming the Government, become Prime Minister and Deputy Prime Minister.

Calls have been made for more clarity to be given to the role.[324] The Prime Minister does have a much greater place in public affairs than other Ministers. That is an essential part of the job – acting as the face of Government to the people. This entails ceremonial and publicity functions. The Prime Minister's key function, however, is to lead the Government. This is done by chairing Cabinet meetings, allocating Cabinet portfolios and exercising some discipline over the Government. Discipline extends from threats and censure, through to dismissal.[325] The ability to assign portfolios has its own disciplinary effect. The incentive of promotion and the fear of demotion in a Cabinet reshuffle are significant.

192. The Prime Minister also has the power to instruct the Governor-General to dissolve Parliament and to hold an early and unexpected election. Usually, this would follow consultation with Cabinet.

193. The Prime Minister's Office is a structure that deals with the political side of the Prime Minister's job, answering letters and determining strategy. The Department of the Prime Minister and Cabinet is a separate entity which researches, coordinates and gives advice to the Prime Minister and Cabinet.

---

320. The Remuneration Authority's job is to fix salaries, allowances and superannuation levels for members of Parliament, the judiciary and some other statutory appointments, including the salary and allowance of the Governor-General. The Authority operates pursuant to the Remuneration Authority Act 1977.
321. Members of Parliament (Remuneration and Services) Act 2013, s. 8(4).
322. Registered under the Superannuation Schemes Act 1989.
323. Remuneration Authority Act 1977, s. 12.
324. G. Palmer, *New Zealand's Consitution in Crisis: Reforming our Political System*, 150–174 (John McIndoe 1992).
325. Rarely used.

§4. Caucus

194. Caucus, the weekly meeting of the parliamentary party, is too cumbersome to provide sophisticated policy analysis. However, it is useful as a sounding board for the Cabinet. The collective responsibility doctrine ensures that Cabinet policies are presented to caucus as a united view. Backbench Members of Parliament are not limited to being a testing area for Cabinet strategies. They are also involved in a caucus committee system. Caucus committees exist in both Opposition and Government caucuses. The caucus committees research matters of a similar nature to Cabinet committees, and report back to caucus. They may require public servants to appear before them.

§5. The State Sector

I. Introduction

195. In New Zealand the State sector comprises Government departments and the State-owned enterprises.

Government departments are bodies set up by statute with the task of advising the Minister who is responsible for the area. The departments are directly responsible to the Minister and are funded from the public purse.

State-owned enterprises are essentially the commercial wing of Government which prior to 1987 existed as State trading organizations,[326] government companies[327] or government corporations[328] and which for reasons of perceived increased efficiency were converted into State-owned enterprises. Many entities which became State-owned enterprises have since been fully privatized.

II. Public Service and the Moves towards Reform

196. Although the policy and direction of the Government are determined largely by the Cabinet, these determinations rely heavily on the advice offered to the Government by the various State sector agencies and departments. Similarly, the

326. These bodies were responsible to a Minister, reported to Parliament and came under the financial control of Government. An example is the Post Office which was governed by the Post Office Act 1959 till 1987, when it became a State-owned enterprise pursuant to the State-Owned Enterprises Act 1986. The Post Office was split into three divisions: New Zealand Post Ltd, Post Office Bank Ltd and Telecom Corporation of New Zealand. These were later privatized.

327. These were set up as private companies and were subject to Companies Act 1955. While these could essentially operate as private companies, the Government retained public ownership by being the major shareholder and typically had representation on their boards. Companies also had to report to Parliament. An example was Air New Zealand.

328. These were typically set up under statutes, and were independently funded. They had therefore the greatest degree of financial independence. Ministers often sat on their Boards, however, and the enterprise still had to report to Parliament. An example was the Tourist Hotel Corporation. For further practical information on the three types of commercial trading arms *see,* J. Ringer, *An Introduction to New Zealand Government* chs 5 and 6 (Hazard Press 1991).

implementation of Government policy initiatives is the task of the public service and related agencies. The public service has, since 1912, been a politically neutral service, dedicated to serving the Government of the day.

197. In 1984, Treasury reported to the Government administration severely criticizing the State sector, citing a paucity of clear goals and measures for effectiveness as reasons for the inefficiency and over-expansion associated with the public service. Similarly, many departments were seen to lack autonomy, with political interference hampering the drive towards efficiency.

198. The reforms then undertaken were therefore directed at improving State sector efficiency. The State sector was totally reviewed. Essentially, all departments were restructured so that their goals and purposes were clearly defined, and so that resources were targeted to goals. A separation was also sought between commercial and non-commercial State activities. The former were mostly reorganized under the State-Owned Enterprises Act 1986, and some enterprises were privatized.[329]

The restructuring of the State sector was confirmed by the State Sector Act 1988. Further changes of a similar kind were effected by the Government's Employment Contracts Act 1991.[330]

199. The Public Service comprises all the departments listed in the First Schedule to the State Sector Act 1988. These departments include Government agencies which provide services from which no profit can be expected,[331] and policy advisory bodies, and investigative and regulatory bodies.[332]

200. The purposes of the State Sector Act 1988 include the promotion of efficiency, the imbuing of the State services with a spirit of service to the community, integrity, responsible management and good employment practice.[333] Chief executives[334] are charged with the efficient, effective and economical management of departmental activities in accordance with duties imposed by law and Government policy.[335] They are appointed for terms not exceeding five years, and negotiate personal employment conditions with the State Services Commissioner although the State Services Commissioner must obtain the agreement of the Prime Minister and

329. State-owned enterprises are discussed more fully later. For discussion on the necessity for reforms *see,* G. Palmer, *Unbridled Power: An Interpretation of New Zealand's Constitution and Government*, 78–90 (2d ed., Oxford U. Press 1987).

330. The Employment Contracts Act 1991 was repealed and replaced by the Employment Relations Act 2000. There are significant differences between the two Acts reflecting the differing policies of Governments led by the National Party (which introduced the Employment Contracts Act) and the Labour Party (which introduced the Employment Relations Act). The Employment Relations Act emphasizes good faith behaviour between the parties in the employment relationship, the presence of unions, and collective bargaining. It also emphasizes mediation as a means of resolving disputes.

331. For example, the Ministry of Education and the Ministry of Social Development.

332. For example, the Treasury, the Serious Fraud Office, and the New Zealand Customs Service.

333. State Sector Act 1988, s. 1A.

334. Section 31.

335. Section 32.

the Minister of State Services before finalizing the conditions of employment with the Chief Executive.[336]

The current mode of appointment of chief executives involves the possibility of political appointments. Although the State Services Commissioner recommends and appoints the chief executive, a Minister may influence and veto the decision. If the chairperson's recommendation is declined, the Governor-General in Council (by convention on the advice of the Minister) may direct the chairperson to appoint someone else in place of the person recommended.[337]

201. The chief executive appoints other staff. These staff are employed pursuant to the Employment Relations Act 2000.

202. Accountability is established in the relationship between the Minister and the chief executive.[338]

203. The allocation of financial resources is covered by the Public Finance Act 1989, and it further increases the reciprocal relationship between Ministers and chief executives. Votes are required each year for the allocation of funding, and must be accompanied by estimates of the money needed for achieving the various outputs necessary for the desired Government outcomes specified by the Minister.[339]

204. The public servant's role is to put Government policies into effect. This is the position, regardless of the politics of the Government. It applies in the economic, regulatory/administrative, welfare, and law and order areas. The public service also assists in creating Government policy by offering advice and information.

III. State-Owned Enterprises

205. The first sectors of the public service to feel the effect of the 1984 commitment to State sector reform were those selected to become State-owned enterprises.

206. The change in the running of these Government enterprises was undertaken because of inherent weaknesses perceived in the State system. Many organizations were the victims of contrary aims: they were required to act profitably, yet they were also subject to political controls.

The State-Owned Enterprises Act 1986 established as the enterprises' primary goal their operation as successful businesses.[340] They were to operate profitably and with efficiency, be good employers, and exhibit a sense of social responsibility. To

336. State Sector Act 1988, s. 38(1).
337. Section 35.
338. Section 32.
339. Section 13.
340. Section 4.

ensure that this principal objective is met, various accountability procedures have been established.

207. It is the role of the directors of a State-owned enterprise to ensure that the aim of being a successful business is pursued.[341] This is implemented in accordance with the enterprise's statement of corporate intent,which is an annual declaration of the enterprise's objectives and position, and includes an outlook for the forthcoming three years.[342] It may also include any information required by the relevant Minister.

208. An audited financial report and a report on the enterprise's operations must also be submitted to the shareholding Ministers each year, as well as a half-yearly financial report.[343] All this information is laid before the House of Representatives by the Minister.[344] The Minister may also request any other information from the board of the enterprise.[345] The purpose of these provisions is to make vital information public and for State enterprises to be accountable to the public through Parliament. Under the Act, State-owned enterprises are declared to be companies under the relevant companies legislation. There is also a special unit within the Treasury called the Crown Ownership Monitoring Unit that monitors the performance of the assets and provides strategic ownership advice to the New Zealand Government on the commercial assets it owns.

209. The shares in a State enterprise are held by the Minister of Finance and the Ministers responsible for the enterprise.[346] The shares cannot be disposed of in any way.[347] However, enterprises may, if authorized by the House of Representatives, issue State enterprise equity bonds.[348] The Ministers who hold shares have some powers. The State enterprises are accountable directly to the Ministers as shareholders.

210. The emphasis on profitability does not preclude State enterprises undertaking non-commercial activities. Where the Crown wishes an enterprise to provide any goods or services, the Crown may enter into an agreement with the enterprise, under which the Crown will pay for or subsidize the enterprise's activities in providing the goods or services.[349] Any compensation that the enterprise seeks from the Crown for the performance of services is to be included in the statement of corporate intent.

---

341. Section 5.
342. Section 14.
343. Sections 15–16. To enhance accountability, the report must contain a comparison between the performance of the enterprise, and the projected performance in the Statement of Corporate Intent.
344. Section 17.
345. Section 18.
346. Section 10.
347. Section 11.
348. Section 12.
349. Section 7.

IV. Privatization

211. In many cases, the restructuring of Government corporations served as a precursor to their sale to private interests, both in New Zealand and abroad. This was the position for instance with Postbank and the Telecom Corporation. Other assets were sold directly to private interests without first going through the process of becoming a State-owned enterprise under the State-owned Enterprises Act 1986.[350]

212. Some sales are made subject to conditions to prevent advantage being taken of a monopoly position. Thus, the sale of Telecom involved a guarantee that standards of service and pricing would be maintained.

V. The Treasury

213. The Treasury is part of the Public Service.[351]

214. The Treasury is responsible for management of Government finances and the preparation of Government accounts. It is also the Government's principal advisor in economic and financial affairs, and it is here that much of its strength lies. The Public Finance Act 1989 has also given statutory expansion to its role, such that it operates the Crown Bank Accounts and monitors the Departmental Bank Accounts.[352] The Act gives power to Treasury to require information allowing it to fulfil its role of financial reporting.[353] Treasury also has the roles of managing the public debt and informing the public on financial matters. Treasury's main influence stems from the fact that all proposals before Cabinet with revenue implications must be considered by Treasury first. Similarly, the Minister of Finance usually provides Treasury with a strong voice in Cabinet.

350. For example, New Zealand Steel and the Rural Bank.
351. State Sector Act 1988, s. 27.
352. Public Finance Act 1989, s. 65R-65W.
353. Sections 79–81.

Chapter 5. The Judiciary

§1. Introduction

215. In New Zealand there are courts of general and special jurisdiction. The work of the general and special courts for the most part uses adversarial process, with barristers and solicitors of the High Court of New Zealand presenting their client's case to the judge, judge and jury, or panel of judges who decide the case on the basis of what is set before them in open court.

216. Tribunals on the other hand typically follow an inquisitorial model. Many tribunals are constituted as Commissions of Inquiry[354] and have the procedural powers of a District Court. Tribunals are viewed as administrative agencies rather than as courts and typically are subject to some degree of control by the courts of general jurisdiction.

217. Alternative models of dispute resolution are increasingly being used. In the Family Court, for instance, there is emphasis on reconciliation with mediation conference facilities and counselling available. A 2014 family justice reform placed even more emphasis on reaching out-of-court settlements about care arrangements for children through a family dispute resolution service. Family dispute resolution involves an independent part facilitating discussion between the parties to a dispute to resolve the dispute. Similarly in the youth area, whole families and invited parties are encouraged to participate in Family Group Conferences to discuss appropriate ways of dealing with the young person in question.[355] As court costs and pressures rise, independent persons are increasingly being called upon by parties to arbitrate or mediate their case out-of-court.

218. There was substantial change in the court system as a result of a Royal Commission Report in 1978.[356] The aim of the report was to improve the efficiency and structure of the courts and generally make reforms which would improve the public perception of the courts. Recommendations adopted included: the renaming of the Supreme Court as the High Court[357] and the renaming of the Magistrates' Courts as District Courts,[358] and the establishment of the Family Court.[359]

354. Pursuant to the Commissions of Inquiry Act 1908. The tribunals may have elements or powers of commissions, but often without the power to award costs. This essentially means that they have the power to order witnesses to appear, to order documents to be produced and to actively search out material and facts to help it decide issues before it. This latter power is wider than the power of a conventional court which is adversarial rather than inquisitorial in its approach.
355. Sections 20–38 of the Children, Young Persons and Their Families Act 1989 provides for family group conferences.
356. *Report of the Royal Commission on the Courts* (Government Printer, Wellington). Also 1978 AJHR H2.
357. Judicature Amendment Act 1979. The name of Supreme Court has been revived as that of the top court by the Supreme Court Act 2003.
358. District Courts Amendment Act 1979
359. Pursuant to the Family Courts Act 1980.

In 1989, the Law Commission produced a report[360] on the structure of the courts. The report was prompted by the increasing workload on the courts, its recommendations included a reallocation of the court's work giving District Courts more power in criminal areas.

219. The courts and tribunals are here considered in three categories:

- ordinary courts (in ascending order);
- special courts;
- tribunals (there are numerous tribunals: the most important will be selected).

§2. Ordinary Courts

I. District Courts

220. District Courts are constituted under the District Courts Act 1947 as courts of record.[361] There are District Courts in over sixty localities.

A. *Judges*

221. Judges are appointed by the Governor-General by warrant. Currently the number of judges cannot exceed 156. An appointee must have held a practising certificate as a barrister and solicitor for at least seven years. Alternatively, they must have been admitted as a barrister and solicitor for not less than seven years and been continuously employed as an officer of the Ministry of Justice for a period of at least ten years, and not less than seven years of that period must be as the Clerk or Registrar of a court.[362] The Governor-General also appoints a Chief District Court Judge.[363] Salaries and allowances of the Chief District Court Judge and other judges is determined by the Remuneration Authority and is payable out of public money without further appropriation.[364] Judges may be removed for inability or misbehaviour and must retire upon reaching the age of 70 years.[365]

---

360. *The Structure of the Courts* NZLC R7. Also 1989 AJHR E 31 D; *see also*, *Delivering Justice for All: A Vision for New Zealand Courts and Tribunals*, NZLC R85.
361. Section 3. For a history of these courts *see*, J.L. Robson, *New Zealand: The Development of Its Laws and Constitution* 71 (2d ed., Stevens and Sons 1967) and J.A.B. O'Keefe & W.L. Farrands, *Introduction to New Zealand Law* 33 (4th ed., Butterworths 1980). The District Courts Rules 2014 regulate the procedure of the District Courts.
362. Section 5.
363. Section 5A.
364. Section 6.
365. Section 7.

B. Jurisdiction

222. The District Court in its civil jurisdiction may hear:

(i) proceedings where the debt, demand or damages or the value of the chattels claimed is up to New Zealand Dollar (NZD) 200,000;[366]
(ii) proceedings for the recovery of penalty, expenses, contribution or demands up to NZD 200,000;[367]
(iii) proceedings for the recovery of land in some circumstances and where the value of the land is not more than NZD 500,000, or where the rent payable does not exceed NZD 62,500 a year;[368]
(iv) disputes between building societies and their members of an amount up to NZD 200,000.[369]

The District Court has the same equitable jurisdiction as the High Court to hear proceedings up to NZD 200,000 and to hear proceedings for the dissolution and winding-up of a partnership whose assets do not exceed NZD 200,000.[370]

Cases relating to amounts in excess of NZD 200,000 may also be brought within the jurisdiction of the District Court if the party abandons the excess,[371] or the parties agree among themselves that the District Court shall have jurisdiction.[372]

There are also provisions for the transfer of cases involving over NZD 50,000 to the High Court on objection by the defendant, and for transfer of cases involving less than NZD 50,000 which involve an important question of fact or law.[373]

Jurisdiction is also conferred on the District Court by a number of other Acts.[374]

There is general right of appeal against a District Court decision.

223. The criminal jurisdiction of the District Courts is prescribed by section 9 of the Criminal Procedure Act 2011. A District Court has jurisdiction to deal with a proceeding for any offence, subject to section 9(2) and (3) and section 114(2) of the Act. Those sections provide that:

(1) The District Courts have jurisdiction in respect of category 2 or 3 offences,[375] unless an order is made under section 68 or section 70 that the proceeding be heard in the High Court. If the trial is to be heard in the High Court, the District

366. District Courts Act 1947, s. 29.
367. Section 30.
368. Section 31.
369. Section 33.
370. Section 34.
371. Section 36.
372. Section 37.
373. Section 43.
374. For example, the Insolvency Act 2006.
375. The categories of offence are defined in s. 6 of the Criminal Procedure Act 2011. Category 2 offences are those punishable by less than two years' imprisonment (or an equivalent offence committed by a body corporate), or an offence punishable by a community-based sentence and not punishable by a term of imprisonment. Category 3 offences at those punishable by imprisonment for life or for two years or more (or an equivalent offence committed by a body corporate).

Courts have jurisdiction until the proceeding is transferred to the High Court under section 75.

(2) The District Courts have jurisdiction in respect of category 4 offences[376] only until the proceeding is transferred to the High Court under section 36 (which it must be after the defendant's first appearance in court).

(3) Where a defendant pleads guilty or if found guilty in a District Court, that Court must transfer the proceeding to the High Court for sentencing of the defendant if section 81B or section 90 of the Sentencing Act 2002[377] apply, or if the offence is a category 4 offence.

II. High Court

224. The High Court is established under the Judicature Act 1908.[378] It is a superior court of record for the administration of justice throughout New Zealand. There is only one High Court but it has several registries and holds regular sittings in many cities.

A. Judges

225. The High Court comprises the Chief Justice of New Zealand and up to fifty-five puisne judges,[379] with provision for additional temporary judges to be appointed when required.[380] All appointments are made by the Governor-General.[381] All appointees must have held a practising certificate as a barrister or solicitor for at least seven years.[382] Salaries and allowances are determined by the Remuneration Authority and are payable out of public money without further appropriation.[383] Judges must retire at the age of 70 years.[384]

---

376. A category 4 offence is one listed in sch. 1 to the Criminal Procedure Act 2011, or an offence of conspiring, attempting, inciting, procuring, or attempting to procure any person to commit an offence listed in sch. 1 to the Act, or being an accessory after the fact to an offence listed in sch. 1 to the Act. Schedule 1 offences include murder, manslaughter and treason.
377. That is, the defendant could be sentenced to life imprisonment or preventive detention.
378. Section 3. The Supreme Court was first established in 1841. It had the same jurisdiction as, and is a colonial successor to, the superior English Courts: Exchequer, Kings Bench, Common Pleas, Probate, Admiralty and Chancery. For details on the early history of the Courts see*:* J.L. Robson, *New Zealand: The Development of Its Laws and Constitution* 77 (2d ed., Stevens and Sons 1967). Rules regulating the practice and procedure of the High Court are the High Court Rules which are promulgated as the Second Schedule to the Judicature Act 1908.
379. Section 4.
380. Section 11.
381. Section 4.
382. Section 6.
383. Section 9A.
384. Section 13.

B. Jurisdiction

226. The Judicature Act 1908 provides that the High Court has 'all judicial jurisdiction which may be necessary to administer the laws of New Zealand'.[385] The court has original and appellate functions. Its jurisdiction is virtually unlimited. In respect of commencement of actions, those which cannot be commenced in a District Court may be commenced in the High Court. Jurisdiction has been extended under a number of statutes.[386]

Proceedings may be transferred to the High Court from the District Court and other inferior tribunals. The High Court also hears appeals from the District Court and some other bodies.

There is an appeal right from judgments of the High Court to the Court of Appeal. The content of the appeal rights will depend on whether the High Court is exercising its original or appellate jurisdiction, and on the nature of the proceeding.

The more serious criminal offences are also dealt with by the High Court generally before a jury.[387]

The powers of the Court may be exercised by one or more judges unless a statute specifically requires a full court or a specific number of judges.

C. Associate Judges of the High Court

227. To assist the High Court judges the Governor-General may appoint no more than nine people who have held a practising certificate as a barrister or solicitor for at least seven years to be Associate Judges of the High Court. An Associate Judge holds office until he or she retires, resigns or is removed from office according to law.[388]

Associate Judges may resign by notice to the Minister of Justice, may be removed for inability or misbehaviour and must retire at the age of 70 years.[389] Their salaries and allowances are determined by the Remuneration Authority and are payable out

385. Section 16. The Court also has an inherent jurisdiction through the Common Law. *See, Nash v. Nash* [1924] NZLR 495. An example is the power to punish for contempt: *see,* the Supreme Court decision in *Vincent Ross Siemer v. Solicitor-General* [2010] NZSC 54, [2010] 3 NZLR 767.

386. For example, the Trustee Act 1956.

387. The jury system in New Zealand is governed by the Juries Act 1981 and the Jury Rules 1990 (SR 1990/226). Persons who are registered as electors may be chosen for jury service: s. 6. There are exemptions and disqualifications under the Juries Act 1981. This includes any person who has been imprisoned for three years or more, any Member of Parliament or any lawyer: ss 7 and 8. Twelve people make up the jury: s. 17. Juries normally sit in serious criminal cases (in some, only where the defendant elects trial by jury), and in civil cases where a party applies and the debt or damage is greater than NZD 3,000 though this is now rare: Judicature Act 1908, s. 19A(2). In practice, a judge will instruct the jury on points of law and may either leave the case to the jury to find for either party or may ask the jury to answer such issues as the judge thinks fit. In a civil case, if after four hours a jury has not come to a unanimous decision, the view of three-quarters of them will be the verdict: s. 29D Juries Act (2008). In criminal cases, under exceptional circumstances, the court may accept a verdict agreed by all except one of jurors: s. 29C Juries Act.

388. Section 26C.

389. Section 26E.

of public money without further appropriation.[390] Associate Judges have and exercise all the powers of High Court judges in relation to a number of civil matters.[391] An Associate Judge can transfer a matter to a High Court judge by reason of its complexity.[392] Review by the High Court of decisions of Associate Judges in their chambers jurisdiction are available,[393] as are appeals to the Court of Appeal against decisions of Associate Judges exercising the jurisdiction of High Court judges.[394] Associate Judges are given the same immunities as a judge of the High Court.[395]

D. Judicial Review

228. The High Court has the power of judicial review of administrative action under the Judicature Amendment Act 1972. On an application for review under the Act of the exercise or non-exercise of a statutory power, the High Court may grant relief to the applicant in the form of a warrant or order of mandamus, prohibition or certiorari, or a declaration or injunction. The Court may, if it finds that the decision made pursuant to the exercise of a statutory power of decision was invalid, set aside the decision rather than make a declaration. The Court may also require the administrative authority to re-consider and re-determine any part of the decision to which the application relates.[396]

229. In 1968, an Administrative Division of the High Court was set up[397] to hear appeals particularly from administrative tribunals.[398] It was abolished in 1991.[399]

E. Commercial List

230. In 1986, the commercial list was set up.[400] The Governor-General may declare a commercial list to be established at any office of the High Court.[401] The aim of the commercial list is to provide a mechanism whereby commercial proceedings can be dealt with expeditiously and efficiently. The proceedings eligible for

390. Section 26F.
391. Section 26I. For example, summary judgment applications and winding-up of companies.
392. Section 26N.
393. Section 26P.
394. That is decisions under s. 26I.
395. Section 26Q.
396. Section 4. *See,* further discussion on judicial review later.
397. Judicature Amendment Act 1968. It inserted ss 25–26B into the Judicature Act 1908. Numerous statutes provided for appeals to the Division. There were up to seven judges who exercised the powers of the Division while retaining the full powers of High Court Judges. The Division had powers under the Judicature Act 1908 to make certain orders. Lay members and assessors could be appointed to sit with the Division in any proceedings where an enactment specified it.
398. Section 26.
399. Judicature Amendment Act 1991.
400. Judicature Amendment Act 1986 inserting s. 24A to 24G.
401. Section 24A. The first has been set up in Auckland.

the commercial list are those with a commercial element.[402] The commercial list is supervised by a High Court judge nominated by the Chief Justice.[403] No commercial list proceeding may be tried by a jury.[404]

F. Cross-Border Proceedings

231. The Judicature Amendment Act 1990 provided for some cross-border jurisdiction between New Zealand and Australia. If the High Court is satisfied that a New Zealand proceeding could more conveniently or fairly be heard in the High Court in Australia, or that evidence could more conveniently be given in Australia, it may order that the proceeding be tried or heard in Australia.[405]

Pursuant to the Agreement between the Government of New Zealand and the Government of Australia on Trans-Tasman Court Proceedings and Regulatory Enforcement signed in July 2008, the New Zealand Parliament passed the Trans-Tasman Proceedings Act 2010 in August 2010. The Act provides for service in Australia of initiating documents for civil proceedings commenced in New Zealand courts and tribunals, the stay of New Zealand civil proceeding on grounds that an Australian court is a more appropriate forum, New Zealand courts granting interim relief in support of civil proceedings in Australian courts, a Trans-Tasman evidence regime involving remote appearance, and recognition and enforcement of judgments of Australian courts and tribunals.[406]

III. Court of Appeal

232. This Court has a very limited original jurisdiction; its main function is as an appellate court. It is established under the Judicature Act 1908, as a court of record.[407] Its seat is in Wellington. It usually sits in divisions of three Judges.[408] The Court sometimes sits with five judges and occasionally with seven.

402. Section 24B. Examples are proceedings relating to commerce and trade, applications under the Arbitration Act 1996 and appeals from determinations of the Commerce Commission.
403. Section 24C.
404. Section 24F.
405. Section 56E. The Trade Practices (Misuse of Trans-Tasman Marketing Power) Act 1990 (C'th) is an Australian law and makes similar provision for the cross-border jurisdiction allowing the Federal Court of Australia to sit in New Zealand.
406. Trans-Tasman Proceedings Act 2010.
407. Section 57. For details of the early history of the Court *see,* J.L. Robson, *New Zealand: The Development of Its Laws and Constitution* 80 (2d ed., Stevens and Sons 1967); J.A.B. O'Keefe & W.L. Farrands, *Introduction to New Zealand Law* 34 (4th ed., Butterworths 1980). The Court of Appeal Rules 1955 (SR 1955/30) regulate the practice and procedure of the Court of Appeal.
408. Section 58.

A. Judges

233. The Court of Appeal comprises a judge of the High Court appointed by the Governor-General to be President, and five to nine other High Court judges appointed by the Governor-General. Office is held as long as the office of judge of the High Court is held.[409] Salaries and allowances are determined by the Remuneration Authority and are payable out of public money without further appropriation.[410] Retirement is at the age of 70.[411] Judges of the Court of Appeal rank higher than all High Court judges, and the judges of the Supreme Court and the President of the Court of Appeal have seniority over the other Court of Appeal judges.[412]

B. Jurisdiction

234. In its civil jurisdiction the Court of Appeal is typically concerned with hearing appeals from judgments, determinations or orders of the High Court.[413]

The High Court may order the removal into the Court of Appeal of any proceedings if the circumstances are exceptional, for example if the proceeding raises a question of law which is the subject of conflicting decisions of the High Court.[414]

An appeal may lie from the Court of Appeal to the Supreme Court.

235. In its criminal jurisdiction the Court of Appeal primarily hears appeals brought to it from the other courts. There is also an original jurisdiction given to the Court of Appeal to try at the Bar criminal cases which are transferred to it from the High Court and involve a matter of extraordinary importance or difficulty.[415]

IV. Supreme Court

236. The Supreme Court Act 2003 created a Supreme Court of New Zealand, to replace the Privy Council as New Zealand's final appellate court. Appeals to the Supreme Court are by leave only.[416]

The Act provides for the Supreme Court to give leave to bring appeals direct from certain decisions of courts other than the Court of Appeal. Unless exceptional circumstances are established, only direct appeals from the Court of Appeal can be heard in the Supreme Court.[417]

409. Section 57.
410. Section 9A.
411. Section 13.
412. Section 57.
413. Sections 66–67.
414. Section 64.
415. Section 69. This is not often used.
416. Section 12.
417. Section 14.

The Supreme Court comprises the Chief Justice and four or five other judges appointed by the Governor-General.[418] The Chief Justice is the head of the New Zealand judiciary, and has seniority over the other judges of the Supreme Court. Judges of the Supreme Court are senior to all other judges.[419]

A judge of the Supreme Court is by definition a High Court judge and holds office on the same terms and conditions as a High Court judge.[420]

§3. Special Courts

237. There are a number of specialist courts in New Zealand. Significant courts are described below.

I. Family Court

238. Family Courts are established under the Family Courts Act 1980 as a division of the District Court.[421] Judges must either be District Court judges or be appointed as such it also appointed as a Family Court judge. In all cases appointees must have the experience, training and personality which makes them suitable for the job. Office is held for the same duration as a District Court judge.[422] A Principal Family Court judge is appointed by the Governor-General and holds office for a period of eight years and is not eligible for reappointment.[423]

The Family Court has jurisdiction under a number of Acts to deal with family law matters, such as separation and dissolution of marriage, adoption, guardianship and domestic protection.[424]

A key principle under the Act is that proceedings are conducted so as to avoid undue formality. As a manifestation of this wigs are not worn in the courts by judges and gowns are not worn by counsel.[425] A Family Court may state a case for the High Court on a question of law, and proceedings may be transferred to the High Court if the proceedings are sufficiently complex to warrant transferral.[426]

---

418. Section 17.
419. Section 18.
420. Sections 20 and 22.
421. Section 4. The Courts were established following recommendations of the *Report of the Royal Commission on the Courts.*
422. Section 5.
423. Section 6.
424. Section 11. For example, jurisdiction is given to determine proceedings under the following Acts: Marriage Act 1955; Adoption Act 1955; Care of Children Act 2004; Domestic Actions Act 1975; Property (Relationships) Act 1976; Family Proceedings Act 1980; Child Support Act 1991; Children, Young Persons and Their Families Act 1989; Law Reform (Testamentary Promises) Act 1949; Family Protection Act 1955; Wills Act 2007; and the Civil Union Act 2004. The Matrimonial Property Act 1976 was significantly revised in 2001 and renamed the Property (Relationships) Act 1976. The coverage of the law now extends to people in de facto relationships, and to the division of property upon death.
425. Section 10.
426. Sections 13 and 14.

II. Youth Court

239. Youth Courts are established under the Children, Young Persons, and Their Families Act 1989 as a division of the District Court.[427] The Chief District Court Judge designates certain District Court judges to be Youth Court judges, taking into account their training and experience, understanding of cultural values and suitability for the work.[428] A Principal Youth Court judge is appointed by the Governor-General and holds office for a period of eight years and is not eligible for reappointment.[429]

The Court has jurisdiction in respect of children and young persons. A child is defined in the Act as a boy or girl under 14 years of age and a young person as a person of 14 years or over and up to 17 years, as long as the person is not married or in a civil union.[430] The Court in general deals with young people who have committed offences other than murder and manslaughter.[431] Where a young person is charged with murder or manslaughter, or has been charged with another offence and elected trial by jury, all applicable pre-trial processes must take place in the Youth Court.[432]

The emphasis in the Act and in the way the Court functions is on mediation and consultation rather than sentencing. Courts exercising powers under the Act are guided by various principles, primarily that the child's or young person's family participate in any decision-making and that decisions be made that will strengthen the child/family bond.[433]

Generally prior to instituting proceedings against a young person a family group conference must be held.[434] This is convened by a Youth Justice Coordinator.[435] The Conference may be attended by a number of people including the child or young person, their family, the Youth Justice Coordinator, the informant, any victim, any barrister, solicitor, and youth advocate or lay person representing the child or young person and a social worker.[436] The conference may formulate plans in respect of the child or young person, including recommending that proceedings be commenced or discontinued.[437] The results of the conference shall be considered by the Court and no order may be made by a Youth Court until a conference has been held.[438]

427. Section 433.
428. Section 435. The designation can extend to Family Court Judges.
429. Section 434.
430. Section 2.
431. Section 272.
432. Section 275.
433. Section 5.
434. Section 245.
435. Section 247.
436. Section 251. Youth Justice Coordinators are covered in ss 323–325 of the Act. They are appointed by the Director-General of Social Welfare to coordinate matters relating to children and young persons and their treatment under the Act. They are available for children and young persons who appear before the Youth Court and who do not already have a lawyer. The appointee must have a background suitable for representing the child or young person. The court may also appoint suitably qualified lay advocates to appear in support of a child or young person who is appearing before a Youth Court.
437. Section 260.
438. Section 281.

Where a charge is proven in a Youth Court a variety of options are open to the Court including discharge, admonition, fine, an order of restitution, an order for community work or supervision.[439]

The young person, or his or her parent or guardian may appeal to the High Court against a finding of a Youth Court only on a question of law.[440]

III. Court Martial; Court Martial Appeal Court

240. The Court Martial of New Zealand is the appellate body for the Armed Forces. As the name suggests, the Court hears matters arising from court martials. It is presided over by judges. Judges are barristers and solicitors who have held practising certificates for at least seven years or are District Court Judges;[441] they are appointed by the Governor-General.[442] The court martial comprises a Chief Judge and at least six other judges.[443] There is a reconsideration procedure under the Armed Forces Discipline Act 1971 for court martial decisions of sentences of imprisonment and detention.[444] There is also a right of appeal under the Court Martial Appeals Act 1953. Appeal can be against decisions relating to bail, against ruling and against conviction or sentencing.[445]

The Court Martial Appeal Court is a superior court of record and has all powers necessary to determine any question and do justice in any case.[446] It consists of High Court judges and barristers and solicitors who have had practising certificates for seven years appointed as judges by the Governor-General.[447]

Appeal to the Court of Appeal or the Supreme Court is available, but only with leave of the court appealed to.[448]

IV. Maori Land Court and Maori Appellate Court

241. The Maori Land Court is a court of record.[449] It sits in seven districts around New Zealand. It has, under the Maori Land Act 1993, all the jurisdiction necessary to hear and determine any claim in law or equity, in respect of ownership or rights in Maori freehold land. This includes any right, title, estate, interest or right of possession or ownership in the land or in the proceeds of the land.[450]

The Governor-General appoints fit and proper persons as judges of the Maori Land Court. Appointees must be barristers and solicitors who have held a practising

439. Section 283.
440. Sections 351–354.
441. Court Martial Act 2007, s. 11.
442. Section 14.
443. Court Martial Act 2007, s. 10.
444. Armed Forces Discipline Act 1971, pt 8.
445. Sections 6–9.
446. Section 4.
447. Section 3.
448. Section 10.
449. Te Ture Whenua Maori Act 1993 (Maori Land Act 1993), s. 6.
450. Section 18.

certificate for at least seven years. The number of judges may not exceed fourteen.[451] A Chief Judge and a Deputy Chief Judge are appointed under the Act.[452]

The Maori Appellate Court is also constituted as a court of record.[453] It comprises the judges of the Maori Land Court, any three of whom may act as the Maori Appellate Court.[454] The Maori Appellate Court has jurisdiction to hear appeals from final orders of the Maori Land Court.[455]

V. Employment Court

242. The Employment Court is governed by the Employment Relations Act 2000. Under the Employment Relations Act 2000, employers and employees come to an agreement on the terms and conditions to be in their contract of employment. The Act encourages the use of mediation to resolve employment disputes, and the Ministry of Business, Innovation and Employment offers a free mediation service.[456] The Act also establishes an authority called the Employment Relations Authority, which is an investigative body with the role of resolving employment relationship problems by establishing the facts and making a determination according to the substantial merits of the case, without regard to technicalities.[457] Generally parties must attempt to resolve their dispute through mediation before the Employment Relations Authority will consider it. The Authority may send the dispute back to mediation.[458] Members of the Employment Relations Authority are appointed by the Governor-General on the recommendation of the appropriate Minister for renewable four-year terms.[459]

The Employment Relations Authority refers questions of law to the Employment Court. The tribunal defers adjudication until the Court's decision on the matter is received. Parties may apply for the removal of proceedings, or appeal to the Court from the tribunal.[460]

The Employment Court is a court of record with powers conferred on it by the 2000 Act and all the powers inherent in a court of record.[461] The court has jurisdiction to hear and determine appeals from adjudications of the Employment Relations Authority, as well as jurisdiction to hear certain types of other employment-related claims under the Act.[462]

451. Section 7.
452. Section 8.
453. Section 50.
454. Section 51.
455. Section 58.
456. Section 144.
457. Sections 156 and 157.
458. Section 159.
459. Section 167.
460. Sections 177, 178.
461. Section 186.
462. Sections 178, 187, 194.

243. The Court consists of the Chief Judge and at least two other judges.[463] Judges are appointed by the Governor-General and an appointee must be a barrister and solicitor who has held a practising certificate for at least seven years.[464] The commissions of all judges remain in force during good behaviour and judges may only be removed by Her Majesty on an address from the House of Representatives.[465] Retirement age is 70 years.[466] Salaries and allowances are determined by the Remuneration Authority without further appropriation.[467]

Appeals are to the Court of Appeal by leave, but only on questions of law.[468] Review of proceedings is also available.[469]

§4. Legal Status of Judges

244. Appointment of judges is non-political. All appointments are made by the Governor-General.[470] The judiciary is independent and is not subject to political interference.[471] A number of factors assist in making an independent judiciary. Appointment is until the retirement age of 70 years.[472] The Supreme Court, the Court of Appeal and High Court judges may not be removed from office other than by the Sovereign or Governor-General acting on an address by the House of Representatives.[473] This may be moved only on the grounds of incapacity or misbehaviour. The removal of District Court judges is statute-based and is on the grounds of misbehaviour or inability.[474] Salaries and allowances of all judges are structured at generous levels eliminating the need for extrajudicial salaries. They are also permanently appropriated.[475] As a further safeguard, the Constitution Act 1986 provides that the salary of a judge of the High Court, Court of Appeal or Supreme Court may not be reduced during their commissions.[476]

245. Supreme Court judges, Court of Appeal judges and High Court judges are, under the common law, absolutely immune from civil proceedings for acts done in the exercise of their judicial office – extending to malicious and careless acts, and as long as jurisdiction is not exceeded. By statute, District Court judges have the

463. Section 197.
464. Section 200.
465. Section 204.
466. Section 205.
467. Sections 171 and 206.
468. Section 214.
469. Section 213.
470. District Courts Act 1947, s. 5; Judicature Act 1908, ss 4 and 57; Supreme Court Act 2003, s. 17.
471. Standing Order 117 of the Standing Orders of the House of Representatives prohibits Members of Parliament from referring to members of the judiciary using offensive words. In practice, however, this has not stopped some politicians from publicly criticizing the judiciary.
472. District Courts Act 1947, s. 7; Judicature Act 1908, s. 13.
473. Constitution Act 1986, s. 23.
474. District Courts Act 1947, s. 7.
475. District Courts Act 1947, s. 6; Judicature Act 1908, s. 9A.
476. Section 24.

same immunities as High Court judges, as do judges of the Employment Court, Maori Land Court, Court Martial, and Associate Judges of the High Court.[477]

246. The Judicial Conduct Commissioner and Judicial Conduct Panel Act 2004 established the office of the Judicial Conduct Commissioner, and authorized the Attorney-General to appoint a Judicial Conduct Panel where necessary. The main function of the Commissioner is to receive complaints about Judges and to deal with complaints as required by the 2004 Act.[478]

§5. Tribunals

I. General

247. There are over 100 different tribunals in New Zealand, all of which have different purposes, and different compositions. The avenues of appeal from tribunals broadly fall into two categories.

248. The first group are appeal bodies which are chaired by judges. The second group consists of bodies with registration, licensing and disciplinary powers over professions, occupations, trades and activities. The membership of these bodies is made up of individuals from the profession or occupation in question.

One such body is the New Zealand Lawyers and Conveyancers Disciplinary Tribunal. It is established under the Lawyers and Conveyancers Act 2006. It consists of a chairperson, a deputy chairperson, and seven to fifteen lay members appointed by the Governor-General on recommendation of the Minister of Justice, and between seven and fifteen lawyers, and three to five conveyancing practitioners appointed by the New Zealand Law Society and the New Zealand Society of Conveyancers respectively.[479] The chairperson and deputy chairperson must not be practitioners but must have had at least seven years' practice as a lawyer.[480] The Tribunal's functions include hearing and determining any application made by a Standards Committee or the Legal Complaints Review Officer for the suspension of a practitioner pending the determination of a charge that the Standards Committee or the Legal Complaints Review Officer has laid against that practitioner, and hearing and determining charges against a practitioner, a law firm or an employee of a law firm laid by a Standards Committee or a Legal Complaints Review Officer.[481]

249. The third category is largely made up of administrative tribunals, many of which are managed by the Ministry of Justice, which provides administrative support services. These tribunals, therefore, are different to the previous mentioned

477. District Courts Act 1947, s. 119; Employment Relations Act 2000, s. 203; Maori Land Act 1993, s. 12A; Court Martial Act 2007, s. 18; Judicature Act 1908, s. 26Q.
478. Judicial Conduct Commissioner and Judicial Conduct Panel Act 2004, s. 8.
479. Lawyers and Conveyancers Act 2006, ss 228, 230 and 233.
480. Section 230.
481. Section 227.

ones, in that they are neither appeal bodies nor profession/occupation-based tribunals. Instead they cover a wide range of areas. A selection is described below.

II. Human Rights Review Tribunal

250. This Tribunal operates under the Human Rights Act 1993, and hears complaints about discrimination.[482] These are usually based on factors such as sex, race, colour, religious or ethical belief, and marital status, in the fields of employment, accommodation and advertising.[483]

The composition of the Tribunal is a chairperson and two other members appointed by the Chairperson for a hearing.[484] The other appointees are chosen from a panel which is maintained by the Minister of Justice. The panel consists of twenty people. People are selected for the panel on the basis of their knowledge, experience and personal attributes.[485]

The chairperson is appointed for a five-year term[486] by the Governor-General on the recommendation of the Minister of Justice[487] and must be a barrister and solicitor of not less than five years' practice.[488] A Deputy Chairperson may also appointed be under the Act.[489]

An office of Human Rights Proceedings established under section 20A decides on the provision of representation in tribunal proceedings, and whether to refer the complaint back to the Human Rights Commission.[490]

The Human Rights Commission provides for dispute resolution services under section 77. These services may include general information about discrimination and legal obligations in relation to discrimination, or providing a venue for, and a mediator at, any dispute resolution meeting that allows each party to discuss and try to resolve a complaint.

III. Tenancy Tribunal

251. The tribunal was established under the Residential Tenancies Act 1986 and consists of Principal and Deputy Tenancy Adjudicators who must be barristers and solicitors having had practising certificates for five years in New Zealand or a common law country. Others are appointed as required; they may be either barristers or solicitors or persons who have special knowledge and experience of tenancy adjudication.[491] A Principal Tenancy Mediator and Tenancy Mediators are appointed

482. Human Rights Act 1993, ss 93 and 94.
483. These are prohibited grounds of discrimination under the Act, as set out in s. 21.
484. Section 98.
485. Sections 98 and 101.
486. Section 100.
487. Section 99.
488. Section 99A.
489. Section 102.
490. Section 90.
491. Residential Tenancies Act 1986, s. 67.

under the Act to try to bring parties to an agreement.[492] If this is not possible, then the Tribunal adjudicates.[493] If a party is dissatisfied with the tribunal's decision it may appeal to a District Court.[494] Appeals from the District Court decision can be made to the High Court and then the Court of Appeal, but on questions of law only.[495]

The Tribunal has the jurisdiction to determine all disputes arising between landlords and tenants in relation to any residential tenancy including determining whether any rent charged exceeded market rent prices; whether any notice terminating a tenancy was authorized; or whether the landlord unreasonably withheld his or her consent to sublet. The tribunal has jurisdiction only to require a tenant or landlord to pay any sum or do any work to the value of NZD 50,000.[496]

IV. Environment Court

252. The Environment Court is a court of record.[497] It consists of a Principal Environment Judge, Environment Judges, alternate Environment Judges and Environmental Commissioners.[498] All are appointed by the Governor-General on the advice of the Attorney-General, who must consult with the Ministers of Environment and Maori Affairs.[499] Environment Judges must be, or be eligible to be, a District Court judge. If they are not a District Court judge at the time of appointment, they will also be appointed as a District Court judge. Alternate Environment Judges must be District Court or Maori Land Court judges.[500] The Resource Management Act 1991 specifies that there are to be no more than ten Environment Judges at a time, but the number of alternate Environment Judges is unlimited.[501] Environmental Commissioners are appointed for their knowledge and experience of matters that may come before the court including economic, local government, planning and scientific knowledge, and knowledge of matters relating to the Treaty of Waitangi and Maori custom.[502]

The quorum for the Environment Court is one Environment Judge and one Commissioner sitting together or one Environment Judge alone for certain purposes or one Environmental Commissioner alone in accordance with the Principal Judge's direction.[503] Special advisors may also be appointed to sit with the court.[504] The Environment Court has the powers of the District Court in procedural matters.[505]

492. Section 76.
493. Section 77.
494. Sections 117–118.
495. Section 119–120.
496. Section 77.
497. Resource Management Act 1991, s. 247.
498. Section 248.
499. Sections 250 and 254.
500. Section 249.
501. Sections 250.
502. Sections 253 and 254.
503. Section 265.
504. Section 259.
505. Section 278.

253. Under the Resource Management Act 1991, there are restrictions on the use of land, subdividing land, the use of coastal marine areas, the use of beds of lakes and rivers, and water.[506] 'Resource consents' are needed to use any restricted resources.[507]

The Court hears appeals from the decision of a consent authority concerning an application.[508] It also has powers to order the taking of land for public works or for heritage protection.[509] Where there are inconsistencies between a national policy statement, a New Zealand coastal policy statement or a water conservation order and a regional policy statement, regional plan or district plan, one of the parties involved may refer the dispute to the Environment Court for its decision. If it finds there is an inconsistency, the Court may order the authority responsible for the policy statement or plan to change it.[510]

254. The Court may state a case for the opinion of the High Court on any point of law that arises in the proceedings. It can adjourn its proceedings until the opinion is given or conclude the proceedings with the opinion.[511]

Decisions of the Environment Court are final unless, due to new and important evidence becoming available or a change in circumstances, there is a rehearing. Appeals to the High Court on points of law are available.[512]

The Environment Court is a procedurally informal body and must recognize customary practices and values where appropriate. It can convene a conference at which the parties are present in order to sort out the issues, the order of proceedings and evidential questions.[513]

Proceedings may be conducted at a place as near to the locality of the subject matter of the proceedings as the Court considers convenient.[514]

V. Commerce Commission and Financial Markets Authority

255. The Commerce Commission has jurisdiction over restrictive trade practices and certain types of mergers and takeovers. It has the power to authorize prices for controlled goods and services.[515] At least one member of the four to six person Commission must be a lawyer and the others must have experience in the areas that the body will deal with – for example in industry, commerce, law and public administration.[516] One of the members must be appointed by the Governor-General as

506. Sections 9–14.
507. Sections 87AA–91C.
508. Section 120.
509. Sections 185–198.
510. Sections 82 and 292–294.
511. Section 287.
512. Sections 294, 295 and 299.
513. Sections 267 and 269.
514. Section 271.
515. Commerce Act 1986, pt 5.
516. Section 9.

Telecommunications Commissioner under the Telecommunications Act 2001.[517] The Commerce Commission has informal investigatory and enforcement functions supplemented by the Fair Trading Act 1986.

The Commission may sit in divisions.[518] There is a right of appeal to the High Court from the Commission's decisions in respect of almost any matter.[519]

256. The Financial Markets Authority is New Zealand's financial markets conduct regulator. Its main objective is to promote and facilitate the development of fair, efficient and transparent financial markets.[520] Under the Financial Markets Authority Act 2011 and the Financial Markets Conduct Act 2013 it licenses and supervises a range of financial service providers and financial products. It also regulates financial markets conduct, monitors compliance, and has various enforcement functions. It may make various enforcement orders under the 2013 Act, including stop orders, direction orders, and orders to prohibit certain disclosure statements being used and various offers being made.[521]

The Authority is established as an independent Crown entity[522] with a Board of between five and nine members.[523] The members are appointed by the Governor-General, on the recommendation of the Minister of Commerce and Consumer Affairs.[524] Up to five associate members may also be appointed.[525] It operates in divisions.[526] The Authority has various general investigation and enforcement powers, may take evidence and have various people appear before it.[527] The Authority may state a case for the opinion of the High Court on a question of law arising in a matter before it. The High Court may remove the matter to the Court of Appeal. The opinion of the court is then to be remitted to the Authority.[528] Appeals to the High Court can be brought against market services licence decisions, and can be brought against various other decision on questions of law only.[529]

517. Section 9(3). Under the Telecommunications Act 2001, the Commerce Commission has specific functions in sector monitoring and information dissemination with regard to the telecommunications market.
518. Section 16.
519. Section 91.
520. Financial Markets Authority Act 2011, s. 8.
521. The Authority's enforcement powers under the Financial Markets Conduct Act 2013 are set out in ss 462–479 of that Act.
522. Financial Markets Authority Act 2011, s. 7.
523. Section 10.
524. Crown Entities Act 2004, s. 28.
525. Financial Markets Authority Act 2011, ss 11–13.
526. This is allowed for by ss 14–16 of the Financial Markets Authority Act 2011.
527. Sections 25–29.
528. Section 48.
529. Financial Markets Conduct Act 2013, ss 531 and 532.

VI. Film and Literature Board of Review

257. The Film and Literature Board of Review is established under the Films, Videos, and Publications Classification Act 1993.[530]

The Board consists of nine members appointed by the Governor-General on the recommendation of the Ministers of Internal Affairs, Women's Affairs and Justice. In appointing members consideration is given to the skill and experience which members have in matters which may come before the Board.[531] Members are appointed for three years and may be reappointed for a further three years.[532] One member of the Board is appointed President. That person must be a barrister and solicitor who has held a practising certificate for at least seven years.[533]

The function of the Board is to review the classification of material under the Act.[534] Applications for review may be made by specified persons who are dissatisfied with classifications.[535] Reviews are conducted as soon as practicable and are by way of re-examination of submitted material, taking into account whether the material is objectionable as it is defined in the Act. Earlier classifications are put aside.[536] The applicant for review and certain other people may make written submissions to the Board. As a result, those people may be invited to attend a hearing but the overall rule is that no one has the right to appear in person before the Board.[537] To carry out its review the Board has powers of consultation.[538] After carrying out its review the Board classifies the material as unrestricted, objectionable or restricted. The Board then gives written notification to the applicant and the Classification Office.[539] It may also state a case on a question of law to the High Court.[540]

VII. Broadcasting Standards Authority

258. The Broadcasting Standards Authority is established under the Broadcasting Act 1989 and deals with complaints relating to broadcasting.[541] Appeal to the High Court is available from the Authority's decisions.[542]

The Authority promotes standards and ethical conduct for broadcasting and encourages broadcasters to consider a number of things (such as portrayal of violence) in their broadcasting particularly in order to protect children. The Authority

530. Section 91.
531. Section 93.
532. Section 94.
533. Section 93.
534. Section 92. This is the material which has already been classified by the Office of Film and Literature Classification established under s. 76 of the Act, pursuant to its s. 77 function.
535. Section 47.
536. Section 52.
537. Section 53.
538. Section 54.
539. Section 55.
540. Section 57.
541. Broadcasting Act 1989, s. 20 and pt 2.
542. Section 18.

is to develop and/or approve codes of broadcasting practice that encourage broadcasters to keep within a certain code.[543]

The Authority may also conduct research and commission programme, audience and technical surveys so as to enable it to perform its functions.[544] There are four members of the Broadcasting Standards Authority, one of whom is a barrister and solicitor with seven years' practice and who is the Chairperson.[545]

For the purpose of any matter before the Authority, the Authority may co-opt any one or more persons whose qualifications or experience are likely to be of assistance to the Authority in dealing with that matter. The co-opted person does not have a right to vote.[546]

VIII. Taxation Review Authority

259. For the purposes of reviewing tax decisions there are special tribunals: the Taxation Review Authorities. Each Authority consists of one person. The person appointed is to be a District Court judge or a barrister and solicitor with seven years' practice. There may be any number of Authorities and each one may be given a distinctive designation as the Governor-General determines.[547]

An Authority has various officers and Registrars to assist him or her to perform the necessary functions of the office.[548] The Authority has the jurisdiction to sit as a judicial authority for hearing and determining objections to tax assessments or against the decisions or determinations of the Commissioner of Inland Revenue.[549]

The Authority is to take an oath before entering his or her office.[550] The Authority has the powers of a Commission of Inquiry except as to ordering costs. It may, however, order costs in certain circumstances set out in the Taxation Review Authorities Act 1994.[551]

Parties appearing before the Authority may be represented by a barrister or solicitor or any other person.[552] Parties may also apply to have a matter stated for the opinion of the High Court. The Authority may also do this on its own motion. The High Court may remove the case stated to the Court of Appeal.[553]

A party may appeal against the Authority's decision where the tax or duty involved is more than NZD 2,000, or if the amount of loss is more than NZD 4,000.[554]

The High Court's decision may be further appealed to the Court of Appeal.[555]

543. Section 21.
544. Section 21.
545. Section 26.
546. Section 26.
547. Taxation Review Authorities Act 1994, s. 5.
548. Section 11.
549. Section 13.
550. Section 7.
551. Sections 15 and 22.
552. Section 16.
553. Sections 24 and 27.
554. Sections 26 and 26A.
555. Section 28.

IX. Waitangi Tribunal

260. The Waitangi Tribunal was established in 1975, with three members, to be chaired by a Judge or a retired Judge of the High Court or the Chief Judge of the Maori Land Court.[556] It developed in part in response to increased Maori protests concerning the breaching of the Treaty of Waitangi signed in 1840. Under section 6 of the initial Act the Tribunal could inquire into claims that were presented to it and make non-binding recommendations to government, concerning legislation or Crown practice or policy that was prejudicial to Maori people and was post-1975. The Tribunal, therefore, did not have much power; nor did it inspire much confidence among the Maori people. By 1984 it had received only fourteen claims and not all of those had been dealt with. The turning point for the Tribunal came when the Tribunal started to conduct its hearings on a marae in the area where the land, fishing rights or other matters were in dispute. Proceedings were in Maori with translation. The first claim to be heard in this way was the Motonui-Waitara Claim.[557] The report came out in 1983. It was the first major case the Tribunal had dealt with. It concerned pollution of Te Atiawa tribe's traditional fishing grounds, by sewage and industrial waste from the Motonui Synthetic Fuel project. The report found that the Te Atiawa fishery would be prejudicially affected by the proposed scheme and that the Crown was obliged to protect these interests under the Treaty of Waitangi.[558]

556. Treaty of Waitangi Act 1975, s. 4. In 1988, the size of the Tribunal was increased so that it could have between two and twenty other members besides the Chairperson.

557. *Report of the Waitangi Tribunal on the Motonui-Waitara Claim* (1983) (Wai 6).

558. The Tribunal's reputation has been further enhanced by subsequent decisions. A selection of key decisions is as follows: *Report of the Waitangi Tribunal on the Kaituna River Claim* (1984) (Wai 4). A plan was formulated to discharge sewage into the Kaituna River. The Tribunal found for the Ngati Pikiao tribe who lodged the claim, and recommended that public money be expended for a land disposal system. *Report of the Waitangi Tribunal on the Manukau Claim* (1985) (Wai 8). Various tribes alleged that use and enjoyment of land was lost through public and private works which had taken place. The Tribunal found for the tribes recommending a return of certain lands to the tribes and an improvement of the Harbour. *Report of the Waitangi Tribunal on the Te Reo Maori Claim* (1986) (Wai 11). The Maori Language Board alleged that Government had not protected the Maori language and sought a variety of assurances to protect the Maori language. This was upheld, Maori language being regarded as taonga. As a result of this claim the Maori Language Act 1987 was passed, recognizing Maori as an official language of New Zealand: s. 3, and allowing Maori language to be used in court: s. 4. *Report of the Waitangi Tribunal on the Muriwhenua Claim* (1988) (Wai 22). The Muriwhenua tribes claimed fishing rights under the Treaty and argued that the right could not be sold to commercial interests. The Tribunal found that the Crown had breached its Treaty obligations in failing to protect Maori fishing rights. *Report of the Waitangi Tribunal on Claims Concerning Allocation of Radio Frequencies* (1990) (Wai 26 and Wai 150). The Tribunal upheld Maori claims objecting to the sale of radio frequencies. *Report on the Crown's Foreshore and Seabed Policy* (2004) (Wai 1071). The Tribunal found that the Crown's policy that reinstated Crown ownership of the Foreshore and Seabed was in breach of Arts 2 and 3 of the Treaty of Waitangi. A Marine and Coastal Area (Takutai Moana) Bill was introduced to Parliament in September 2010 and repealed the Foreshore and Seabed Act 2004. *Ko Aotearoa Tenei* (2011) (Wai 262). The Tribunal reported on the so-called flora and fauna claim, which also dealt with intellectual indigenous property. This was the first whole-of-government report, and the Tribunal made recommendations for wide-ranging reforms to laws and policies affecting Maori culture and identity. It was also the first Tribunal report to consider what the Treaty relationship might become after historical grievances are settled.

261. In 1985, there was a legislative change that increased the Tribunal's membership to seven, four of whom were to be Maori, and also extended the Waitangi Tribunal's jurisdiction retrospectively to 1840. The Tribunal can now hear claims presented by a person of Maori descent on their own behalf or for their tribe claiming that a Crown practice or policy or an Act or regulation since 1840 prejudicially affected them and that the legislation or policy or practice was inconsistent with the principles of the Treaty of Waitangi.[559]

262. In 1986, the State-Owned Enterprises Bill[560] was proposed to enable the Crown to transfer land to State-owned enterprises. As this law would have made it difficult for the Government to return land to Maori people when Tribunal reports recommended such action, two sections were added to the Act: one to protect any claims being considered by the Tribunal at the time of promulgation of the Act and one which laid down that nothing in the Act was to permit the Crown to act in a manner which could be construed as inconsistent with the principles of the Treaty of Waitangi.[561]

263. This legislation gave rise to some confusion, and was the subject of litigation in *New Zealand Maori Council v. Attorney-General*.[562] The result of that case was that the Court of Appeal prohibited the Government from proceeding with sales to State-owned enterprises without court-approved agreement with the complainants. Such sales would violate the principles of the Treaty of Waitangi. The Court of Appeal, in its decision, recognized the Treaty as having, by virtue of the Act, a fundamental constitutional character.

In 1988, the Government enacted the Treaty of Waitangi (State Enterprises) Act 1988 which allows the Tribunal to make binding recommendations for the return of Maori land transferred to State-owned enterprises.[563] The Tribunal's numbers have also been increased to twenty-one.[564]

264. The Tribunal is deemed to be a Commission of Inquiry, but essentially does not act in a formal or traditional judicial manner.[565] Parties are not required to file documents setting out the case before proceedings start. Research of the claim is carried out by Tribunal staff. The Crown is then given time to prepare its defence, once the questions to be settled have been decided.

265. The Tribunal has gained status and recognition through its decisions and is now seen as the main body for settling these types of actions. The decisions of the Tribunal are not binding on the Government except to the extent that claims are affected by the Treaty of Waitangi (State Enterprises) Act 1988. The Tribunal is not

559. Treaty of Waitangi Amendment Act 1985, s. 3(1).
560. Later became the State-Owned Enterprises Act 1986.
561. State-Owned Enterprises Act 1986, ss 27 and 9.
562. [1987] 1 NZLR 641.
563. Treaty of Waitangi (State Enterprises) Act 1988, s. 4.
564. Treaty of Waitangi Act 1975, s. 4.
565. Treaty of Waitangi Act 1975, s. 4 and sch. 2.

a court and cannot make conclusive determinations on legal issues. Despite this, many recommendations have been acted on by the Government.

X. Disputes Tribunals

266. The Disputes Tribunals[566] have taken some of the civil disputes workload off the District Court. The Tribunals have jurisdiction to hear and determine claims which do not exceed NZ Dollar (NZD) 15,000. The claim may relate to work done or to the recovery of property.[567]

In practice they deal with many consumer complaints against suppliers and tradespeople and provide a low cost and efficient method of dealing with minor disputes. If the parties agree, the Tribunal's jurisdiction may be extended to claims not exceeding NZD 20,000; alternatively, a claimant may abandon so much of a claim as exceeds NZD 15,000 to bring it within the Tribunal's jurisdiction.[568]

Disputes Tribunals are presided over by a referee. Referees are appointed by the Governor-General. They are typically people who on the basis of their knowledge, experience and personal attributes are suited to the post. They do not have to be legally qualified.[569] Candidates must be approved by an assessment panel.[570]

Parties are generally not permitted legal representation before the Tribunal but may present their own cases.[571] The referee seeks to bring the parties to an agreed settlement. If that is not possible the referee will come to a decision according to the substantial merits and justice of the case, having regard to the law but not necessarily adhering to legal forms and technicalities.[572] An appeal may be made to the District Court from a decision of a tribunal.[573]

XI. Public and Government Inquiries

267. The Governor-General by Order in Council may establish a public inquiry to inquire into and report on any matter of public importance.[574] One or more

566. Originally established as Small Claims Tribunals by the Small Claims Tribunals Act 1976, these are now provided for in the Disputes Tribunal Act 1988. They are divisions of the District Court: s. 4.
567. Sections 10 and 11.
568. Sections 13 and 14.
569. Section 7.
570. Section 8.
571. Section 38.
572. Section 18.
573. Section 50.
574. Inquiries Act 2013, s. 6(2). Previously such inquiries were called commissions of inquiry and regulated by the Commissions of Inquiry Act 1908. While that Act has not been repealed (because it has been used over the years to give inquisitorial power to many other statutory bodies such as the Waitangi Tribunal), commissions on inquiry can no longer be established under that Act. The new Act came about in response to a 2008 Law Commission report: *A New Inquiries Act* (NZLC R102).

Ministers may, by notice in the Gazette, establish a government inquiry for the purpose of inquiring into, and reporting on, any matter of public importance.[575]

268. An inquiry has the power to obtain information as it thinks appropriate for the purposes of the inquiry, and to summons witnesses.[576] It may state a case to the High Court on any question of law arising in any matter before the inquiry.[577]

An inquiry, the members of an inquiry, and officers of an inquiry have immunity from liability for anything done, reported, stated or omitted in the exercise of powers and performance of duties of the inquiry, unless they acted in bad faith.[578] Furthermore, witnesses have the same immunities and privileges as if they were appearing in civil proceedings.[579]

575. Section 6(3).
576. Sections 20 and 23.
577. Section 34.
578. Section 26.
579. Section 27.

Chapter 6. Independent Non-political Agencies

§1. Advisory and Supervisory, Non-political Agencies: Quangos

269. A host of independent or semi-independent agencies exist which provide advice or services for the Crown. Such agencies are found across the total spectrum of society, in fields as diverse as marketing, culture and arts, planning, transportation, recreation and tourism. These include tribunals and review authorities performing quasi-judicial functions, commissions regulating activities and boards promoting industries. Generalization about these bodies is difficult and they are grouped under various names: 'statutory and allied organizations', 'public advisory bodies', 'statutory bodies','associated organizations' and 'Crown Entities'. Less officially they are known as *quangos* – quasi-autonomous non-governmental organizations.

270. No standard form exists for the establishment of advisory boards.[580] Some are created by legislative authority under their own statute. Usually, the statute establishes the body concerned, sets out its functions, powers, responsibilities and/or privileges, makes provision for members and staff, specifies financial procedures and controls for the body. Thus, for example, under the Law Commission Act 1985, the Law Commission is established as a Crown entity with between three and six Commissioners. It is charged with the systematic review of New Zealand law, given the power to research, review law and conduct hearings as is necessary to maintain and review New Zealand law, and required to report annually to the Minister of Justice.[581]

271. Other more general statutes have similar provisions establishing bodies to perform the functions and achieve the objectives of that statute. Thus, the Human Rights Act 1993 seeks to advance human rights in accordance with the International Covenant on Civil and Political Rights, and contains provisions about unlawful discrimination. To achieve its goals the Act establishes two separate, independent agencies. The Human Rights Commission is formed as a Crown entity to promote and make reports on human rights, as well as investigating and mediating in alleged unlawful discrimination, and in refused applications for membership of unions and organizations such as trade associations. The Act also creates the Human Rights Review Tribunal which adjudicates in cases involving allegations of discrimination.

272. These bodies obtain their funding in different ways. For example, some receive their funding out of the vote of the department to which they are responsible. There are also sections of the Public Finance Act 1989 concerned with the

580. The Legislation Advisory Committee did not favour general umbrella legislation for public advisory bodies. Rather it encouraged ministerial use of common law powers to establish advisory committees, and sought to restrict statutes to those bodies which needed statutory authority for the conferment of powers upon them: *see*, Legislation Advisory Committee, *Public Advisory Bodies* (Department of Justice 1990).

581. Law Commission Act 1985 ss 3–9, 15 and sch. 1.

funding accountability of Crown entities. Section 2 speaks of entities which the Crown is able to control, yet which are not departments, State-owned enterprises or Offices of Parliament. The Crown may make capital payments to Crown entities and obtain any profit an agency may make.[582] The entities must present financial reports so that they are accountable to Parliament.[583] There are also some quangos and boards which are partially or wholly self-funding.[584]

§2. Organs of State Control

I. Audit

273. In New Zealand the body which monitors government spending is the Controller and Auditor-General. The Controller and Auditor-General is an officer of Parliament and a corporation sole with perpetual succession and a seal of office.[585] The Public Audit Act 2001 also provides for the Deputy Controller and Auditor-General who is also an officer of Parliament.[586] The Deputy Auditor-General has and may exercise, to the same extent as the Auditor-General, all the functions, duties and powers of the Auditor-General, subject to the control of the Auditor-General.[587]

274. The Auditor-General and Deputy Auditor-General are appointed by the Governor-General on the recommendation of the House of the Representatives.[588] Salary and allowances of the Auditor-General and Deputy Auditor-General are determined by the Remuneration Authority.[589] The Auditor-General and Deputy Auditor-General may be removed or suspended from office only by the Governor-General pursuant to an address from the House of Representatives for reasons of disability affecting the performance of duty, bankruptcy, neglect of duty or misconduct.[590] The Auditor-General may appoint auditors or delegate powers to an employee of the Auditor-General.[591]

275. The Auditor-General is the auditor of every public entity and carries out financial report audit, performance audit and other auditing services.[592] It may also audit other entities at those entities' request.[593] For carrying out the functions, duties and powers, the Auditor-General has powers to obtain information from an entity or

582. Public Finance Act 1989, ss 15 and 16.
583. Public Finance Act 1989, s. 41. Crown entities include the Crown health enterprises and the Crown research institutes.
584. For example, the Standards Association of New Zealand is a fully commercial operation, with its basis in the Standards Act 1988.
585. Public Audit Act 2001, ss 7(1) and 10.
586. Section 11.
587. Section 12.
588. Sections 7(2) and 11(2).
589. Schedule 3, cl. 5.
590. Schedule 3, cl. 4.
591. Sections 32–35.
592. Sections 14–17.
593. Section 19.

a person who has custody, care or control of that information or document, to examine on oath, to inspect bank accounts, to access premises, and to disclose information that the Auditor-General considers appropriate to disclose.[594]

276. For every financial year the Auditor-General must prepare and present an annual report to the House of Representatives in accordance with section 43 of the Public Finance Act 1989,[595] and in addition must report at least once every calendar year to the House of Representatives on matters arising out of the performance and exercise of the Auditor-General's functions, duties and powers.[596] In the Annual Report the Auditor-General notes any irregularities and shortcomings discovered.

277. Under the Public Finance Act 1989, the Auditor-General also has the power to direct a Minister to report to the House of Representatives if the Auditor-General has reason to believe that expenses or capital expenditure for which that Minister is responsible have been incurred for a purpose that is not lawful or not within the scope, amount or period of any appropriation, or other authority, by or under an Act.[597] The Auditor-General may also stop payment out of a Crown Bank Account or a Departmental Bank Account for the same reasons.[598]

II. Reserve Bank

278. The Reserve Bank is the central bank of New Zealand. Among its functions are the issuing of New Zealand's notes and coins and monitoring the country's financial institutions. It has a Banking Supervision Department to supervise registered banks to ensure they comply with certain standards. The Reserve Bank may require information from these banks and, if a registered bank fails, is responsible for the statutory management of the failed bank.[599]

Other functions are to be a lender of last resort, to act as a financial products registration service and to carry on the business of banking including the Government's banking business.[600]

279. The Reserve Bank's primary function is to formulate and implement the country's monetary policy – that of maintaining price stability.[601] In formulating the policy the Bank has regard to the financial system and consults with bodies which can assist it to maintain economic objectives.[602]

594. Sections 24–30.
595. Section 37.
596. Section 20.
597. Public Finance Act 1989, s. 65Z.
598. Section 65ZA.
599. Reserve Bank of New Zealand Act 1989, ss 25–30 and 117–140. A registered bank is one which is registered under the Act: ss 2 and 69.
600. Sections 31–39.
601. Section 8.
602. Section 10.

The Minister of Finance and the Governor of the Reserve Bank must agree on policy targets, in order to assist the Bank in achieving the monetary policy of price stability. These are set for the term of the Governor.[603]

It is the Governor's duty, under the Act, to ensure that any action the Bank takes to keep prices stable are consistent with the policy targets set.[604] The targets may be changed on consultation with the Minister, and if a new economic objective other than price stability is declared, new policy targets are to be fixed.[605] In implementing the monetary policy the Reserve Bank may continue to operate in the financial markets, buying and selling Reserve Bank Bills, Treasury Bills and Government Securities.

280. Every six months, or more frequently at the Minister's direction, the Bank must produce and publish a policy statement for the next six months.[606]

III. Ombudsmen

281. In 1962, the Parliamentary Commissioner (Ombudsman) Act introduced a constitutionally important office to New Zealand and to the non-Nordic world. The office of Ombudsman was adopted from Scandinavia and adapted to the New Zealand system of government. The Office is presently provided for and governed by the Ombudsmen Act 1975.[607]

The Ombudsmen's Office was established because of the need by the public for a body which could examine public grievances against government agencies, particularly those grievances which could not easily be resolved by other mechanisms such as the courts.

282. Provision is made in the Act for the appointment of one or more Ombudsmen. The Ombudsmen are officers of Parliament, and are responsible to Parliament, not to the Government. They are appointed by the Governor-General on the recommendation of the House of Representatives[608] for a term of five years, and can only be removed from office by the Governor-General, on an address from the House, for inability to perform the functions of the office, bankruptcy, neglect of duty or misconduct.[609]

---

603. Section 9. The Reserve Bank has a Governor, appointed for five years to ensure the Bank carries out the functions imposed by the Act: ss 40 and 42. One or two Deputy Governors are also appointed: *see,* s. 45. Under the 1989 Act the Board of Directors constituted under s. 52 have become a monitoring body – providing guidance and monitoring the performance of the Bank and the Governor in the execution of duties: s. 53. The Board consists of five to seven non-executive directors appointed by the Minister of Finance, and the Governor: s. 54.
604. Section 11.
605. Sections 9 and 12.
606. Section 15.
607. *See also,* the Ombudsmen Rules 1989 (SR 1989/64).
608. Section 3.
609. Sections 5 and 6. There are currently two Ombudsmen with a staff of sixteen investigators.

283. The jurisdiction of the Ombudsmen is provided for in the Act:[610]

> it shall be a function of the Ombudsmen to investigate any decision or recommendation made, or any act done or omitted ... relating to a matter of administration and affecting any person or body of persons in his or its personal capacity...

The Act covers acts and omissions of a variety of bodies covering central government departments and organizations and quangos, listed in the First Schedule to the Act.

284. The procedures for investigations are informal and inexpensive. Proceedings are conducted in private. The Ombudsmen have full powers to consult and obtain information. No person has an entitlement as of right to be heard.[611] Powers are given to Ombudsmen to require the furnishing of documents and other evidence, and they may summon people and examine on oath.[612] Information may not have to be provided, however, where its disclosure would prejudice New Zealand's security, defence or international relations or make public certain Cabinet proceedings.[613]

285. The Ombudsmen may refuse to hear complaints where the complainant has not exhausted available legal remedies. The Ombudsmen also have a discretion not to investigate cases which are trivial, frivolous or vexatious, made in bad faith or where the complainant does not have a sufficient interest in the matter. The Ombudsmen may also cease to investigate claims which turn out not to require further investigation.[614]

286. The Ombudsmen have power of recommendation only; they do not have a power to decide.[615] Their role is essentially conciliatory. The primary emphasis is on the need to resolve differences by discussion and negotiation, rather than assigning responsibility for administrative failure or apportioning blame.

287. The Ombudsmen's office is now firmly established in New Zealand. Numerous complaints are received from members of the public each year.[616] If the

610. Section 13(1).
611. Section 18.
612. Section 19.
613. Section 20.
614. Section 17.
615. Section 22.
616. For the year ended June 2014, the Ombudsmen received 2,478 complaints under the Ombudsmen Act 1975 and 6,032 other contacts concerning matters under that Act, 1,027 complaints under the Official Information Act 1982 and 246 complaints under the Local Government Information and Meetings Act (*Ombudsman Annual Report for the year ended 30 June 2014* presented to the House of Representatives pursuant to s. 29 of the Ombudsmen Act 1975).

Ombudsmen reach an unfavourable view of a decision complained of, they can recommend and report that:[617]

(i) the matter be referred to the appropriate authority for further consideration;
(ii) the decision be cancelled, varied or rectified;
(iii) any practice on which the decision was based be altered;
(iv) the law on which the decision was based be reconsidered;
(v) the reasons for the decision be given; or
(vi) any other steps be taken.

Although the Ombudsmen's recommendations are not binding, the effectiveness of the office and the esteem in which it is held is shown by the fact that the recommendations are rarely rejected.

288. If no adequate action is taken by the department concerned in response to the Ombudsmen's recommendation, the Ombudsmen can report the matter to the Prime Minister and then report to Parliament as they see fit.[618] The complainant must also be kept informed of the outcome of any investigation that has taken place.[619] The report of the Ombudsmen's office is tabled annually in Parliament.[620] A compendium of cases investigated, recommendations made and the results is also published each year.

IV. Official Information

289. The Official Information Act was passed in 1982.[621] Official information is widely defined: it means any information held by a department, or a Minister in his or her official capacity, or an organization, and includes any information held outside New Zealand by any branch or post of a department or an organization.[622]

290. The 1982 Act repealed the Official Secrets Act 1951, which was based on a United Kingdom statute of the same name. The 1951 Act began with the presumption that official information belonged to the Government and would not be given out unless there was good reason.

291. The purposes of the 1982 Act are quite different:[623]

(a) to increase progressively the availability of official information to the people of New Zealand in order:

617. Section 22(3).
618. Section 22(4).
619. Section 24.
620. Section 29.
621. *Towards Open Government*, Report of the Committee on Official Information (Government Printer 1981). On the issue of freedom of information generally, *see*, I. Eagles, M. Taggart & G. Liddell, *Freedom of Information in New Zealand* (Oxford U. Press 1992).
622. Official Information Act 1982, s. 2.
623. Section 4.

(i) to enable their more effective participation in the making and administration of laws and policies; and
(ii) to promote the accountability of Ministers of the Crown and officials – and thereby to enhance respect for the law and to promote the good government of New Zealand.

(b) to provide for proper access by each person to official information relating to that person;
(c) to protect official information to the extent consistent with the public interest and the preservation of personal privacy.

292. The Act works on the basic presumption that the information requested shall be made available[624] unless there is a specified public interest reason under the Act for withholding it. Conclusive reasons[625] for withholding information are that disclosure is likely to:

(i) prejudice New Zealand's defence or security or the Government's international relations;
(ii) prejudice the entrusting of confidential information to the New Zealand Government by other governments or international agencies;
(iii) prejudice the maintenance of law and order and the right to a fair trial;
(iv) endanger the safety of any person;
(v) damage the economy of New Zealand.

A special provision exists covering New Zealand's associated States. It provides that information may be withheld if its disclosure would prejudice the security or defence of the Cook Islands, Niue, the Ross Dependency or Tokelau, or the governmental and international relations of any of them.[626]

293. Other reasons which will prevent disclosure unless there are considerations which make it desirable in the public interest to release the information[627] include:

(i) to protect individual privacy;
(ii) to protect commercial information;
(iii) to protect certain types of confidential information;
(iv) to avoid prejudice to the public safety;
(v) to avoid prejudice to the economic interests of New Zealand;
(vi) to maintain various constitutional conventions;
(vii) to maintain the conduct of public affairs;
(viii) to maintain legal professional privilege;
(ix) to enable the Crown to carry on negotiations.

624. Section 5.
625. Section 6.
626. Section 7.
627. Section 9.

294. Any person who is a New Zealand citizen, resident or is in the country and anybody corporate incorporated in New Zealand or with a place of business in New Zealand may request official information from a department, Minister of the Crown or organization.[628] Those from whom the material is requested must then within twenty days decide whether to release the material and if so convey it to the applicant.[629] All departments, Ministers and organizations are obliged under the Act to assist those who request official information.[630] Where documents are involved, releasing the information may involve allowing inspection or providing a copy of the document or other summary of its contents. Reasons must be provided if the documentary information is not provided in the requested manner.[631]

295. Apart from statutory provisions in the Official Information Act 1982 justifying the withholding of information, requests for official information may also be refused if:

(i) making the information available would be contrary to the principles of a specified enactment or constitute a contempt of Parliament;
(ii) the information will soon be publicly available;
(iii) the request is made by a defendant or a person on behalf of a defendant and is for information that could be sought by the defendant under the Criminal Disclosure Act 2008;
(iv) the document containing the information does not exist or cannot be found;
(v) the information will require substantial collation or research;
(vi) the information is not held by the department, Minister or organization;
(vii) the request is frivolous or vexatious.[632]

Where a request is refused reasons for the refusal must be given.[633]

296. The Act also provides for a right of access to personal information. Every person has a right to access to personal information which is held about that person and which can readily be retrieved. The provision is qualified – it can only be exercised by a person who is a body corporate incorporated in New Zealand, or a body corporate incorporated outside New Zealand but with a place of business in New Zealand.[634]

---

628. Section 12.
629. Section 15.
630. Section 13.
631. Section 16.
632. Section 18.
633. Section 19.
634. Section 24. Personal information is defined in the Act as any information about an identifiable person: s. 2. Access to personal information about natural persons is provided in the Privacy Act 1993.

297. Apart from the statutory provisions justifying the withholding of information, there are provisions in the Act justifying refusal to disclose personal information. Information may be refused if the request is frivolous or vexatious or the information requested is trivial or if the disclosure:[635]

(i) would be likely to prejudice any of the interests protected by sections 6(a)-(d), 7 and 9(2)(b);[636]
(ii) would involve the unwarranted disclosure of the affairs of another person or of a deceased person;
(iii) being evaluative material,[637] would breach a promise made to the supplier of the material;
(iv) would breach legal professional privilege.

298. The Ombudsman may review decisions under the Act.[638] If disclosure is recommended by the Ombudsman there is a public duty on the Minister, department or organization to comply with the requirement within twenty-one days.[639]

299. The Ombudsman's decision is subject to the Governor-General's veto by Order in Council.[640] That Order in Council must be published in the *Gazette* and se

635. Section 27(1).
636. These sections read:

> ***6 Conclusive reasons for withholding official information*** Good reason for withholding official information exists, for the purpose of section 5, if the making available of that information would be likely—(a) to prejudice the security or defence of New Zealand or the international relations of the Government of New Zealand; or (b) to prejudice the entrusting of information to the Government of New Zealand on a basis of confidence by—the Government of any other country or any agency of such a Government; or any international organisation; or(c) to prejudice the maintenance of the law, including the prevention, investigation, and detection of offences, and the right to a fair trial; or (d) to endanger the safety of any person; ...
>
> ***7 Special reasons for withholding official information related to the Cook Islands, Tokelau, or Niue, or the Ross Dependency*** Good reason for withholding information exists, for the purpose of section 5, if the making available of the information would be likely— (a) to prejudice the security or defence of—(i) the self-governing State of the Cook Islands; or (ii) the self-governing State of Niue; or (iii) Tokelau; or (iv) the Ross Dependency; or (b) to prejudice relations between any of the Governments of—(i) New Zealand: (ii) the self-governing State of the Cook Islands: (iii) the self-governing State of Niue; or (c) to prejudice the international relations of the Governments of—(i) the self-governing State of the Cook Islands; or (ii) the self-governing State of Niue.
>
> ***9 Other reasons for withholding official information*** ... (2) ... (b) protect information where the making available of the information—(i) would disclose a trade secret; or (ii) would be likely unreasonably to prejudice the commercial position of the person who supplied or who is the subject of the information; ...

637. Evaluative material is evaluative or opinion material gathered to determine the award, continuation, modification or cancelation of contracts, awards or other benefits, or insurance purposes: s. 27(2).
638. Section 28.
639. Section 32.
640. Section 32.

out the reasons for which it was made.[641] The making of the Order in Council itself may be subject to review in the High Court and after that to appeal in the Court of Appeal.[642]

300. The Local Government Official Information and Meetings Act 1987 are similar to the 1982 Act. It applies the same principle of open government to local authorities, providing for access to official information held by those bodies.[643]

V. Privacy

301. The Privacy Act 1993 sets up a statutory regime for regulating an individual's privacy. The Act provides twelve guiding privacy principles. These are:[644]

(1) Personal information[645] is not to be collected by an agency[646] unless it is lawful, relevant and necessary.
(2) Personal information is generally to be collected directly from the individual concerned.
(3) The individual from whom personal information is collected is to be informed of the reason and purpose for which it is collected and its intended audience.
(4) Personal information is not to be collected unlawfully or unfairly.
(5) Personal information is to be safely stored and not to be disclosed without authorization.
(6) An individual is entitled to access to the information.
(7) An individual is entitled to have personal information corrected.
(8) Personal information is to be checked for accuracy before it is used.
(9) Personal information is not to be retained longer than necessary.
(10) Personal information gathered for one purpose shall not be used for another purpose unless certain circumstances exist such as that the information is publicly available.
(11) Personal information is not to be disclosed unless the circumstances listed in (10) exist.
(12) Unique identifiers[647] are not to be assigned to individuals unless they are necessary.

641. Section 32A.
642. Section 32B and 32C.
643. For an application of this Act in the courts *see, Wyatt Co (NZ) Ltd v. Queenstown-Lakes District Council* [1991] 2 NZLR 180.
644. Section 6.
645. This is defined in s. 2 of the Act as information about an identifiable individual.
646. Agency is defined in s. 2 of the Act as any person or body of persons, incorporated or unincorporated, in the public or private sector including Departments.
647. This is defined in s. 2 as any identifier assigned by an agency to an individual for the operations of the agency.

Many of the principles contain a standard set of derogations[648] and the Act provides for certain circumstances in which breaches of the guiding principles will be justified,[649] and there are certain exemptions.[650]

302. In respect of principle 6, the Act provides that an agency may refuse to disclose information where it threatens the security, defence or international relations of New Zealand[651] or where it would disclose trade secrets or prejudice commercial transactions.[652] Apart from principle 6 which confers legal rights which are enforceable, none of the guiding principles are enforceable in a court of law.[653] There are, however, safeguards in the Act. Each agency is responsible for appointing a privacy officer or officers who are responsible for privacy matters within the agency, including ensuring compliance with privacy principles.[654] There is also provision under the Act for complaints to be made to the Privacy Commissioner by individuals who believe that their privacy has been interfered with.[655] The complaint may then be investigated by the Privacy Commissioner after notification is given to the complainant and other parties.[656] In some cases complaints may not be proceeded with,[657] or may be more suitably dealt with by an Ombudsman.[658] It may also be possible to procure an almost immediate settlement of a complaint.[659] The Commissioner is empowered to call compulsory conferences to resolve the dispute and has the power to summon persons to attend.[660]

303. After a complaint is investigated and found to have substance, the Commissioner may try to secure a settlement of the complaint, or may refer it to the Director of Human Rights Proceedings[661] for a decision as to whether civil proceedings should be brought against an offender before the Human Rights Review

648. For example, principles 2 and 10 may be derogated from if the information is publicly available: s. 6.
649. For example, where it may be in the public interest for the information to be collected and used: s. 54.
650. Under s. 46 of the Act the Privacy Commissioner may issue codes of practice which modify the application of privacy principles in respect for example of certain types of agencies. There are also certain specific exemptions, for example information held by intelligence agencies: s. 57.
651. Section 27. The wording of this section is similar in substance to that contained in s. 6 of the Official Information Act 1982.
652. Section 28. Other reasons are also provided for in the Act which justify a refusal to disclose information under principle 6: s. 29. These are similar in substance to ss 18 and 27 of the Official Information Act 1982.
653. Section 11.
654. Section 23.
655. Section 69. The Privacy Commissioner is a corporation sole and a Crown entity under the Crown Entities Act 2004. The appointment of Commissioner and deputy Commissioner is governed by the Crown Entities Act 2004: s. 12. The functions of the Privacy Commissioner are extensively specified in s. 13 of the Act, but in summary the functions are to oversee the entire system.
656. Section 73.
657. Section 71.
658. Section 72.
659. Section 74.
660. Section 76.
661. The Director of Human Rights Proceedings is appointed under the Human Rights Act 1993.

Tribunal.[662] It is also open to aggrieved individuals to bring proceedings against an offender if for example the complaint has been found not to have substance.[663] The Human Rights Review Tribunal has powers under the Act to grant remedies including:

(i) a declaration that there has been an interference with privacy;
(ii) an order restraining the defendant from continuing with the interference or requiring the defendant to remedy the interference;
(iii) awarding damages against the defendant.[664]

304. The Act regulates information matching between certain agencies, and authorizes such data matching subject to certain conditions. The Act provides that no personal information held by a specified agency[665] is to be disclosed to another specified agency pursuant to an information matching legislative provision, for comparison, except where it is pursuant to a written agreement between the agencies. The written agreements must incorporate information matching rules and a copy of the agreement must be forwarded to the Privacy Commissioner.[666] It is then possible for adverse action to be taken against an individual on the basis of discrepancies identified by the comparison.[667] Adverse action can include the refusal, cancellation or suspension of monetary payments. Some safeguards are provided by the Act. For example, information derived from a comparison must be destroyed within sixty days if adverse action is not taken and notice must be given to individuals against whom adverse action is proposed.[668]

There are also various reporting requirements imposed by the Act on agencies which are involved in information matching, to report to the Privacy Commissioner,[669] and on the Privacy Commissioner to include in the annual report, details on information matching.[670]

662. Sections 77 and 82. The Human Rights Review Tribunal is established under the Human Rights Act 1993.
663. Section 83.
664. Section 85.
665. Specified agencies are set out in s. 97 of the Act. They include the New Zealand Customs Service, the Ministry of Business, Innovation and Employment, the Ministry of Education, and the Inland Revenue Department.
666. Section 99.
667. Section 100.
668. Section 101.
669. Section 104.
670. Section 105.

Part III. The State and Its Subdivisions

Chapter 1. Local Self-Government

305. Local self-government has two forms in New Zealand. One relates to the relationships of the countries in the Realm of New Zealand. The other relates to the territorial jurisdiction of local administrations within the country.

Chapter 2. Component States

306. New Zealand has had responsibility, both before and since independence in 1947, for the administration of several islands and dependencies. Currently, New Zealand has administrative responsibility for Tokelau and the Ross Dependency in Antarctica. There also exists a special relationship between New Zealand and the Cook Islands, and Niue. The Realm of New Zealand comprises Tokelau, the Ross Dependency, Niue, the Cook Islands and New Zealand.[671]

§1. New Zealand Proper

307. The country comprises the land normally associated with New Zealand and several outlying islands: The Chatham Islands group lies some 850 km to the east, Campbell Island 590 km to the south, and Raoul Island in the Kermadec group 930 km to the north-east.

§2. Tokelau

308. Tokelau[672] comprises three coral atolls, situated 483 kilometres north of Western Samoa and 3,200 kilometres from New Zealand. The atolls (Atafu, Nukunonu and Fakaofo) comprise reef-bound islets each with a central lagoon. Atafu is 3.5 km^2, Nukunonu 4 km^2 and Fakaofo 4.7 km^2.

The population of approximately 1,500[673] is predominantly Polynesian and has close links with Samoa and Tuvalu. 7,176 Tokelauan people live in New Zealand.[674]

It is likely that Tokelau has been inhabited since at least 1000 AD with earliest settlers originating from Samoa, Rarotonga and Tuvalu. During the eighteenth century various sightings were made of Tokelau and in 1841 an American explorer landed on the islands.

Missionary activity commenced about 1845 and by 1863, Atafu was entirely Protestant, Nukunonu Catholic, and Fakaofo a mixture of both faiths. The population was substantially reduced by Peruvian slave raids in 1863.

---

671. *See,* Letters Patent Constituting the Office of the Governor-General of New Zealand, SR 1983/225, as amended by SR 1987/8 and SR 2006/224.
672. For background information on Tokelau *see,* N. Douglas, *Pacific Islands Yearbook* (17th ed., Fiji Times Ltd 1994), 619. For legal information on Tokelau see: A.H. Angelo, *Tokelau,* in *South Pacific Islands Legal Systems,* 296 (M. Ntumy ed., U. Hawaii Press 1993); Rosemary Gordon, *Tokelau – A Collection of Documents and References Relating to Constitutional Development* (2d ed., Tokelau Administration 1995); Tony Angelo & Talei Pasikale *Tokelau: a Hisotry of Government* (Council for the Ongoing Government of Tokelau 2008). Many of the documents referred to are found in Rosemary Gordon's book.
673. In the 2013 population count, the de jure usually resident population count was 1,383.
674. These figures were recorded in the latest (2013) census.

309. In 1877, the Western Pacific Order in Council extended British jurisdiction to Tokelau. This Order gave the British High Commissioner for the Western Pacific jurisdiction over British subjects on Tokelau and set up a system for government of British subjects living in Pacific islands which had not come within the control of any other foreign power. The Order did not typically extend to the native inhabitants of the islands. In 1889, the three atolls of Tokelau became a British Protectorate and were administered by Britain. In 1916,[675] Tokelau was annexed to the Gilbert and Ellice Islands Colony. That colony was already administered by Britain.[676] In 1925, the New Zealand Government agreed to administer Tokelau from Western Samoa which was then a mandated territory of New Zealand. In 1926, Tokelau was excised from the boundaries of the Gilbert and Ellice Islands Colony[677] and administrative control for the islands was transferred to New Zealand.[678] Administrative power was then delegated to the Administrator of Western Samoa.[679]

In 1946, Tokelau was listed by the United Nations as a dependent territory administered by New Zealand. From 1 January 1949, pursuant to the Tokelau Act 1948, Tokelau was incorporated into New Zealand.[680]

310. After 1949 some New Zealand law was extended to Tokelau, although New Zealand law only applies if specifically extended.[681] Law is extended either by regulation made under the Tokelau Act 1948, or by express provision in an Act. All amendments to, and regulations made under the Acts extended are also in force in Tokelau.[682] The Tokelau Act 1948 makes special provision for the Governor-General to make regulations for Tokelau's peace, order and good government.[683] By virtue of section 3A of the Tokelau Act 1948, introduced by the Tokelau Amendment Act 1996, the General Fono (a representative meeting of the three islands) has power to legislate for the peace, order and good government of Tokelau. This latter procedure has become the main method for making law applicable to Tokelau. Under the Tokelau Village Incorporation Regulations 1986, each individual village has power to legislate for the village.[684]

311. Due to its size, remoteness and paucity of resources, Tokelau is heavily dependent on New Zealand.

312. Responsibility for the administration of Tokelau is vested in the Administrator of Tokelau who is based in Wellington. The Administrator has delegated most of his administrative authority to the representatives of Tokelau in Tokelau. The

675. Order in Council Annexing the Union Islands to the Gilbert and Ellice Islands Colony 1916.
676. Gilbert and Ellice Islands Order in Council 1915.
677. Union Islands (No. 1) Order in Council 1925.
678. Union Islands (No. 2) Order in Council 1925.
679. Union Islands (Revocation) Order in Council 1948.
680. Section 3.
681. Section 6.
682. Section 7.
683. Section 4.
684. A.H. Angelo, *Tokelau Village Rules – 1988*, QUTLJ 21 (1988).

Public Service is the largest employer in Tokelau, and is responsible for education, agriculture and fisheries, health, public works, economic development, finance and administration.

313. At the local level, government is in the hands of the Taupulega (council of elders), comprising elders and family heads, together with the elected Faipule and Pulenuku. These latter offices are filled by triennial elections, conducted on the basis of universal adult suffrage. The Faipule for each atoll represents the atoll externally, while the Pulenuku is responsible for village affairs and work.

314. Tokelau-wide government is provided by the meetings of the General Fono. At the General Fono, delegates from each atoll meet to discuss issues affecting Tokelau. Usually, the General Fono meets thrice yearly. When it is not in session the Council for the Ongoing Government exercises executive power for Tokelau.

315. Judicial functions are organized under the Tokelau Amendment Act 1986. That Act provides for the appointment of a Commissioner for each atoll.[685] The Commissioner has civil and criminal jurisdiction in cases involving up to NZD 1,000 or offences punishable by one year's imprisonment, and may impose penalties of up to three months in prison or fines of NZD 150.[686] The parties involved may also agree to allow the Commissioner's jurisdiction, even if it involves an amount beyond that with which the Commissioner may deal ordinarily. Appeals on important matters lie from decisions of the Commissioner to the High Court of New Zealand and from there to the Court of Appeal of New Zealand.[687]

316. Tokelau is a non-self-governing territory under the Charter of the United Nations. The United Nations Special Committee on Decolonisation has visited Tokelau five times – most recently in 2002.

§3. Ross Dependency

317. Since 1923, New Zealand has purported to exercise some degree of jurisdiction over the Ross Dependency in Antarctica. This area comprises about 170,000 square miles of land, and about 130,000 square miles of permanent ice-shelf. The exact extent of New Zealand's authority over the region is something of a moot point in international law. Nevertheless, it is regarded as part of New Zealand for constitutional purposes.

685. Section 5.
686. Section 7.
687. Section 10.

318. The taking of jurisdiction over the Ross Dependency was effected by a British Order in Council of 1923.[688] Under this Order, the King of the United Kingdom gave the Governor-General of New Zealand power and authority over the Dependency. Thus, in the Letters Patent Constituting the Office of Governor-General of New Zealand,[689] Her Majesty makes reference to Her Realm of New Zealand as comprising '… (e) The Ross Dependency'.

Pursuant to the Ross Dependency Regulations 1923,[690] the Governor-General of New Zealand provides for the laws (past and future and including the common law) in force in New Zealand to be extended to the Ross Dependency.

319. There is no general statutory recognition of the Ross Dependency in New Zealand law. Under the Citizenship Act 1977, anyone born in the Dependency is held to be a New Zealand citizen if one of their parents is a New Zealand citizen.[691] There is also the Antarctica Act 1960. By virtue of that Act, the courts of New Zealand are given jurisdiction to try crimes committed in the Ross Dependency.[692] The Act also sets out the Antarctic Treaty to which New Zealand is a party. The Treaty seeks to ensure the use of Antarctica for peaceful purposes, and cooperation between parties. The Antarctica (Environmental Protection) Act 1994 sets up a comprehensive regime to protect the Antarctic environment and implements the Protocol on Environmental Protection to the Antarctic Treaty.

320. New Zealand's presence on the Antarctic continent is very small. A permanent scientific research programme is maintained at Scott Base on Ross Island, and New Zealand also operates two seasonal bases. The New Zealand presence in the Dependency depends heavily on cooperation with the American base at nearby McMurdo Sound. New Zealand annually appoints Officers of the Government of the Ross Dependency to represent the Executive Government. They are senior staff at Scott Base. They are empowered to take all steps necessary or expedient to enforce the laws and regulations in force in the Ross Dependency.

§4. Niue and the Cook Islands

321. Both Niue and the Cook Islands are self-governing States in free association with New Zealand. This has been the Cook Islands position since 1965, and that of Niue since 1974.

---

688. Order in Council providing for Government of Ross Dependency 1923 (*New Zealand Gazette* 1923, vol. II, 2211).
689. Letters Patent Constituting the Office of the Governor-General of New Zealand, SR 1983/225, as amended by SR 1987/8 and SR 2006/224, cl. I.
690. *New Zealand Gazette* 1923, 2815.
691. Citizenship Act 1977, ss 2 and 6. The Citizenship Amendment Act 2005 limits citizenship by birth to people born before 1 Jan. 2006.
692. Antarctica Act 1960, ss 3–5.

I. The Cook Islands

322. The Cook Islands[693] comprises fifteen islands approximately 4,500 kilometres south of Hawaii. The largest island is Rarotonga which is situated approximately 3000 kilometres north-east of Auckland. Rarotonga covers 67 km^2. The second largest island, Mangaia, is 51 km^2. In total the islands cover no more than 240 km^2, and the sea area of the country is approximately 1,830,000 km^2.[694]

The population is predominantly Polynesian. The resident population of the Cook Islands was recorded at the census in 2011 as 17,794. 61,839 Cook Islanders were recorded as living in New Zealand in the 2013 census.

There is evidence of settlement from about 600 AD. It is believed that inhabitants came from Samoa and French Polynesia. The first contact with Europeans occurred in 1595. Missionary activity occurred from 1823 and by the 1860s the islands were Christianized.

Prior to European contact each island ran a separate administration based on the chiefly system. However, in 1888 Rarotonga was declared a British Protectorate which encompassed all the Southern Islands and was known as the Federation of the Cook Islands.

In 1900, Rarotonga petitioned New Zealand to annex the Cook Islands and annexation occurred in 1901.[695]

323. The Cook Islands was governed first under the Cook and Other Islands Government Act 1901. That Act provided that in general the laws in force at the commencement of the Act, including native customary law, remained in force. New Zealand law was not in force unless it was introduced.[696] A Federal Parliament and any Native Councils continued in existence. The various councils were given power, subject to the Governor's veto, to make ordinances for the inhabitants within their jurisdiction.[697] The islands were administered by a Resident Commissioner.[698]

Under the Cook Islands Act 1915, a Legislative Council was set up in Rarotonga, called the Island Council of Rarotonga. Other islands were granted Island Councils at the Governor's discretion.[699] The composition of the Island Council was largely also at the Governor's discretion and contained provision for ex officio members,

693. For background information on the Cook Islands see, *Laws of New Zealand* Pacific States and Territories: Cook Islands (online ed); N. Douglas, *Pacific Islands Yearbook* 83 (17th ed., Fiji Times Ltd 1994); D. Stanley, *South Pacific Handbook* 248 (5th ed., Moon Publications Inc. 1993). For legal information and background information on the Cook Islands *see,* I. Adzoxornu, *The Cook Islands*, in *South Pacific Islands Legal Systems* 3 (M. Ntumy ed., U. Hawaii Press 1993) and Rosemary Gordon, *Cook Islands and Niue: A Collection of Legislation Relating to Constitutional Development* (Port Vila, Vanuatu: USP Complex, 1995).

694. The Southern Islands are Rarotonga, Mangaia, Atiu, Mitiaro, Mauke, Aitutaki, Manuae, Palmerston and Takutea. The Northern Islands are Penhryn, Manihiki, Pukaputa, Rakahanga, Nassau and Suwarrow.

695. Order in Council altering the boundaries of the Colony of New Zealand 1901.

696. Sections 2 and 3.

697. Sections 7 and 8.

698. Section 5.

699. Sections 59 and 60.

including the Resident Commissioner.[700] Island Councils had a limited law-making power.[701]

By 1946, a Legislative Council for the Cook Islands was established comprising members elected from the Island Councils, a number of public servants and the Resident Commissioner. The Resident Commissioner was given the power to make Ordinances of the Cook Islands, with the advice and consent of the Legislative Council.[702]

In 1957, an Executive Committee consisting of the Legislative Assembly, appointed by the Resident Commissioner, was set up to advise the Resident Commissioner.[703] The Legislative Council of the Cook Islands was abolished and replaced by the Legislative Assembly of the Cook Islands. This consisted of members elected by universal suffrage by the electors of all the islands, and some members elected by the Island Councils. There was also a European elected representative and several officials.[704] A law-making power was given under the Act.[705] In 1962, the Resident Commissioner was empowered to delegate powers to the Executive Committee.[706]

324. New Zealand was therefore responsible for the administration of the Cook Islands until the passing, in 1965, of the Cook Islands Constitution Act 1964 (NZ). Under that Act, the Cook Islands was provided with its own Constitution, such that it had full executive, legislative and judicial competence: 'The Cook Islands shall be self-governing.'[707] Nevertheless, the Queen in right of New Zealand could still have responsibility under the Act for the external affairs and defence of the Cook Islands after consultation with the Cook Islands.[708] The Cook Islands are also part of the Queen's Realm of New Zealand in accordance with the 1983 Letters Patent.[709]

Cook Islanders are, if born in the Cook Islands or New Zealand to a New Zealand citizen parent, New Zealanders under the Citizenship Act 1977 (NZ).[710]

325. New Zealand's responsibility for the external affairs and defence of the Cook Islands is flexible.[711] The 'free association' notion means that the Cook Islands can change its relations with New Zealand at any time it chooses. New

700. Sections 62–69.
701. Sections 70–71.
702. Cook Islands Amendment Act 1946, ss 24.
703. Cook Islands Amendment Act 1957, s. 8.
704. Section 32.
705. Section 38.
706. Cook Islands Amendment Act 1962, s. 15, substituting new ss 8 to 11 in the 1957 Amendment Act.
707. Cook Islands Constitution Act 1964, s. 3.
708. Section 5.
709. Letters Patent Constituting the Office of the Governor-General of New Zealand, SR 1983/225, as amended by SR 1987/8 and SR 2006/224, cl. I.
710. Citizenship Act 1977, ss 2 and 6.
711. For a discussion of the practical application of that section *see,* A. Frame, *The External Affairs and Defence of the Cook Islands – the 'Riddiford Clause' Considered*, 17 VUWLR 141 (1987). *See also,* the New Zealand Court of Appeal case *Controller and Auditor-General v. Sir Ronald Keith Davison*, 16 Feb. 1996, CA 226/95. *See also*, the Joint Centenary Declaration of the Principles of the Relationship between New Zealand and the Cook Islands (Rarotonga, 11 Jun. 2001).

Zealand stressed this to the United Nations during the decolonization process. The Cook Islands does exercise autonomy in foreign affairs. It is a member of various international organizations in its own right, particularly at a regional level, where the reality of its independence is more truly recognized. These include the Secretariat of the Pacific Community and the Pacific Islands Forum.

326. The Cook Islands has a legislature of twenty-five members.[712] Elections are held every five years.[713] There is also the House of Arikis, a consultative body of hereditary chiefs, whose authority is especially valued on traditional issues.[714] Cabinet consists of the Prime Minister and between six and eight other Ministers.[715] The Cook Islands has a High Court comprising a civil division, a criminal division and a land division; and a Court of Appeal.[716] There is the possibility of appeals to Her Majesty the Queen in Council.[717]

327. A public service, headed by a Public Service Commissioner who is responsible for appointment, promotion and related matters, is established under the Constitution.[718] The Constitution also makes provision for the protection of human rights including the right to life, liberty and security of the person, and the right of the individual to equality before the law.[719]

II. Niue

328. Niue[720] is a single elevated coral atoll 480 kilometres east of Tonga and 560 kilometres southeast of Samoa. The island has a land area of 258 km^2. At its highest point the land rises to 65 metres above sea level, at its lowest 27 metres above sea level.

The population is predominantly Polynesian. The resident population in Niue is approximately 1,611,[721] and 23,883 Niueans reside in New Zealand.[722]

There is evidence of settlement from about 1000 AD, probably by Samoans and later from Tonga and the Cook Islands. The first European contact was in 1774 with

712. Constitution of the Cook Islands, Art 27.
713. Article 37.
714. Articles 8–11B.
715. Article 13.
716. Articles 47 and 56.
717. Constitution of the Cook Islands, Art 59; Privy Council (Judicial Committee) Act 1984 (CI).
718. Articles 72–76.
719. Article 64.
720. For background information on Niue see, N. Douglas, *Pacific Islands Yearbook*, 467 (17th ed., Fiji Times Ltd 1994); D. Stanley, *South Pacific Handbook* 292 (5th ed., Moon Publications Inc. 1993). For legal information and documents on Niue *see,* A.H. Angelo, *Niue*, in *South Pacific Islands Legal Systems*, 158 (M. Ntumy ed., U. Hawaii Press 1993) and Rosemary Gordon, *Cook Islands and Niue: A Collection of Legislation Relating to Constitutional Development* (USP Complex 1995).
721. According to Niue's 2011 population and household census.
722. According to the 2013 census.

a visit from Captain Cook. Missionary activity occurred from 1830 and by 1854 the island was Christianized. Peruvian slave raids took place in 1863.

In 1876, Niueans elected a King who later petitioned the British Monarch to have Niue declared a British Protectorate. The petition was granted in April 1900. In 1901, Niue was annexed to New Zealand.[723]

329. In the early part of its history Niue was governed under the Cook and Other Islands Government Act 1901 and the Cook Islands Act 1915.[724] In 1957, the Island Council of Niue was abolished and the Niue Assembly was established. It comprised the Resident Commissioner and up to sixteen members appointed by the Governor-General.[725] It was granted a limited law-making power.[726] By 1964, the composition of the Assembly was changed to provide for an Assembly comprising the Resident Commissioner and fourteen members elected by the villages of Niue.[727] An Executive Committee consisting of the Resident Commissioner and four members elected from the Niue Assembly was established.[728] Provision was made for delegation of some of the Resident Commissioner's powers to the Executive Committee.[729] After the Cook Islands became self-governing in 1965, the Niue Act 1966 was promulgated. The Act made extensive provision for the laws and Government of Niue and confirmed the existence of the Niue Assembly and the executive government of Niue.[730] In 1971, executive government of Niue was vested in the Executive Committee directly rather than by delegation.[731]

330. In 1974, the people of Niue voted to become a self-governing State in free association with New Zealand. Niue has a similar constitutional relationship with New Zealand to that of the Cook Islands. It is referred to in the Letters Patent as part of the Realm of New Zealand.

Under the Niue Constitution Act 1974 (NZ), Niue is self-governing,[732] although Her Majesty the Queen in right of New Zealand may retain responsibilities for Niue's external affairs and defence.[733] Nevertheless, Niue has the official constitutional standing necessary to engage in its own foreign relations. It is primarily paucity of resources which prevents it from doing so. It does, however, like the Cook Islands, belong to many regional bodies.

331. Under the Niue Constitution Act 1974, the rights of Niueans to New Zealand citizenship are guaranteed.[734] The Niue Constitution Act 1974

723. Order in Council altering the boundaries of the Colony of New Zealand 1901.
724. Niue was, however, granted a separate administration pursuant to the Cook and Other Islands Amendment Act 1903.
725. Cook Islands Amendment Act 1957, s. 67.
726. Section 69.
727. Cook Islands Amendment Act 1964, s. 31.
728. Section 9.
729. Section 10.
730. *See*, for example ss 4–14 and 31.
731. Niue Amendment Act 1971, adding new s. 8 to the Niue Act 1966.
732. Niue Constitution Act 1974, s. 3.
733. Section 6.
734. Section 5.

requires the Government of New Zealand to provide 'necessary economic and administrative assistance to Niue'.[735] The Act requires that effect be given to this provision, and that consultation occur whenever cooperation between the countries is needed.[736]

332. Niue's Constitution is a Schedule to the Niue Constitution Act 1974 (NZ). The Constitution provides for a twenty member Legislative Assembly. Fourteen of the members come from village constituencies, while the remainder are elected from a common national roll.[737]

333. The Constitution provides for a Cabinet consisting of the Premier of Niue and three other members of the Niue Assembly. The Premier must command the support of the Assembly before proceeding to appoint the other Cabinet members.[738] To help the Cabinet in exercising its executive functions, the Constitution provides also for the functions of the Niue Public Service. The Service is designed to be free from political interference.

334. The judiciary of Niue is constituted under Part III of the Niue Constitution. This creates a High Court with a civil division, a criminal division and a land division.[739] The courts are staffed by the Chief Justice, Judges and Commissioners.[740] Appeals are to a Court of Appeal of Niue.[741] The judges are guaranteed salary and tenure by the Constitution.[742]

735. Section 7.
736. Section 8.
737. Article 16.
738. Articles 2–5.
739. Article 37.
740. Articles 39 and 46.
741. Article 52. Appeals to the Privy Council are also possible: Art. 55.
742. Articles 42–45.

Chapter 3. Local Government

335. The first comprehensive piece of local government legislation was the Municipal Corporations Act 1867, which aimed to standardize local government. In 1876, the provinces were abolished and local government became more important with central government assuming responsibility for local government. In that year the Municipal Corporations Act 1876 brought all existing municipalities under the Act's purview and provided for the establishment of boroughs.

336. The Counties Act 1876 divided New Zealand into sixty-three counties. These counties had elected councils. This was the origin of the system of local government in New Zealand which remained until 1974 when the Local Government Act of that year was enacted,[743] providing for regional government and the establishment of district councils and community councils. By 1989 New Zealand had 205 elected territorial authorities.[744]

337. In 1989,[745] major organizational changes were implemented for the local government regime. In 2002[746] further changes were instigated, dividing the country into local authorities that consisted of regional councils and territorial authorities.[747] Every part of New Zealand, other than the Chatham Islands[748] that is within the district of a territorial authority, has to be within the region of one or more regional councils.[749]

338. The Local Government Act 2002 repealed much of the Local Government Act 1974. The main change is that the Act grants a wide general power to local authorities. They are bodies corporate and section 12 states that 'for the purpose of performing its role, a local authority has full capacity to carry on or undertake any activity or business, do any act, or enter any transaction'.

The Act also emphasizes the accountability of local authorities[750] and their duty to consult.[751] This consultation must include consultation with Maori. Under the Act local authorities must provide processes and opportunities for Maori to contribute to decision-making processes.[752] There has also been increased recognition of Maori on the Local Government Commission: one member must have knowledge

743. The 1974 Act repealed the Municipal Corporations Act 1954 and the Counties Act 1961 which previously governed the areas.
744. *New Zealand Official 1990 Yearbook* (94th ed., Department of Statistics 1990).
745. Local Government Amendment Act (No. 2) 1989.
746. Local Government Act 2002.
747. Local Government Act 2002, s. 21(1).
748. The Chatham Islands has a territorial authority under the Chatham Islands Council Act 1995.
749. Local Government Act 2002, s. 21(2).
750. Local Government Act 2002, s. 14.
751. Sections 82–83A and 86–87.
752. Sections 81–82.

of tikanga (Maori custom and practice), and that member is to be appointed after consultation with the Minister of Maori Affairs.[753]

There were further changes to the Act in 2012, which altered the purpose of local government slightly, aimed to encourage greater financial discipline, and provided new assistance and intervention options to the Minister of Local Government.

339. Territorial authorities are split into districts and cities and take responsibility for the day-to-day provision of services to their local communities. They have functions imposed by statute in relation to water and sanitary services, libraries and parks.[754]

Local authorities are also empowered to corporatize or contract out services or establish a council-controlled organization in which the local authority typically retains 50% or more of the shareholding.[755] A principal objective of a council-controlled organization is to exhibit a sense of social and environmental responsibility by having regard to the interests of the community.[756]

§1. Purposes of Local Government

340. The purposes of local government are defined in the Local Government Act 2002:[757]

> The purpose of this Act is to provide for democratic and effective local government that recognises the diversity of New Zealand communities; and, to that end, this Act –
>
> (a) states the purpose of local government; and
> (b) provides a framework and powers for local authorities to decide which activities they undertake and the manner in which they will undertake them; and
> (c) promotes the accountability of local authorities to their communities; and
> (d) provides for local authorities to play a broad role in meeting the current and future needs of their community for good-quality local infrastructure, local public services, and performance of regulatory functions.

Central Government continues to maintain police, social welfare, education, firefighting and most housing. Local bodies may, however, form joint operations with the central Government for services such as roading and provincial airports.

341. Local government powers are delegated by Parliament under a number of Acts, the primary one being the Local Government Act 2002. As New Zealand has

753. Section 33. However, the Government refused to reserve Maori seats for the Auckland Super City which was established in 2009: *see,* s. 8 of the Local Government (Auckland Council) Act 2009.
754. Local Government Act 2002, s. 123.
755. Sections 56 and 6.
756. Section 59.
757. Section 3.

no written constitution these powers are not inviolable. However, the central government has largely refrained from interfering with the decisions and processes of local government, and local bodies themselves are less concerned with party politics than with their own localities, as is reflected in the number of independent members compared to those with particular party allegiances.

342. Partially as a reflection of restructuring of central and local government, local authorities must function in a market place economy. The Act requires that local authorities conduct their affairs so that their business is conducted in a manner which is clear and comprehensible to the public, and pursuant to clearly stated objectives. It must measure its performance regularly, and keep its local community and in some instances the central government informed of its activities.[758]

343. Each local authority must adopt financial systems which are consistent with generally accepted accounting practices in New Zealand, as well as establishing bank accounts and funds to ensure that its finances are properly managed.[759]

344. The Minister of Local Government has power to request information from a council about a problem and the steps that are being taken to deal with it;[760] appoint a Crown Review Team to investigate a significant problem in a council and make recommendations on how to address it;[761] appoint a Crown Observer to monitor a council's progress on addressing a significant problem and help the council address the problem;[762] appoint a Crown Manager to direct a council to the extent necessary to resolve a significant problem;[763] and appoint a Commission to perform and exercise a council's responsibilities, duties and powers.[764] The Minister can also call a general election of a local authority on specified grounds.[765]

345. There are also extensive reporting requirements set up by the Act. First, in each financial year, a local authority must prepare a report which assesses the performance of the local authority against its stated objectives and fund sources. It must set out its financial statements and include the auditor's report on its financial statements. The report must include statements for any local authority trading enterprise in which the local authority has a financial interest.[766]

Additionally, each local authority must have a long-term plan at all times, which covers a period of not less than ten consecutive financial years, and describes the

758. Local Government Act 2002, s. 14.
759. Section 111.
760. Section 257.
761. Sections 258 and 258A.
762. Sections 258B and 258C.
763. Sections 258D and 258E. In July 2013, following the revocation of the Christchurch City Council's accreditation as a Building Control Authority, a Crown Manager was appointed on the invitation of the Christchurch City Council. The Manager managed the Council's building control functions, reviewed its building consent operations, and advised on the changes necessary for the Council to regain accreditation.
764. Sections 258F to 258L.
765. Section 258M.
766. Sections 98 and 99.

activities of the local authority, provides a long-term focus for the decisions of the local authority, and provides a basis for accountability of the local authority to the community.[767] Each local authority must also adopt an annual plan for each financial year.[768]

Both the financial and planning reports must be made available for the public to inspect and copies must be sent to the Secretary for Local Government, the Auditor-General and the Parliamentary Library.[769]

Council-controlled organizations are also required to deliver to shareholders annual reports, which include a statement of intent as well as a statement of performance of the organizations against their statement of intent, and audited financial statements.[770]

Council-controlled organizations must also prepare half-yearly statements of operations.[771]

346. The local government Acts provide for local authorities to make bylaws and rules on an extensive range of subjects – for instance regulating building, libraries and street traders. They are not to exceed the powers given to the local authority, nor breach the general law, nor be unreasonable. Local body decisions are challengeable in the courts.[772]

347. There is also power for local bodies to levy rates (a form of land tax) and raise loans.[773]

§2. Local Body Elections

348. Local body elections occur triennially, on the second Saturday in October.[774] All regional council, territorial authority, special purpose, local board and community board elections are conducted at the same time. Territorial authorities decide whether the election will be conducted by post or at polling stations.[775]

349. Every parliamentary elector is also qualified as a residential elector for a regional council, a district or a community. There is also provision for qualification of those residing outside the area but who have rate payer qualifications.[776]

767. Section 93.
768. Section 95.
769. Sections 93, 95 and 98.
770. Sections 67 to 69.
771. Section 66.
772. Local Government Act 2002, ss 143–161.
773. Pursuant to the Local Government (Rating) Act 2002.
774. Local Electoral Act 2001, s. 10.
775. Section 36.
776. Local Electoral Act 2001, s. 20.

In general all parliamentary electors are able to stand as candidates for local authorities. There is a restriction on people standing concurrently for a regional council and a territorial authority, local board or community board.[777]

350. Section 27 of the Local Electoral Act states that a local authority may, not later than 12 September in the year that is two years before the year in which the next general election is held, resolve to use a different electoral system from that used in the previous election. If an authority makes such a resolution, it will use a different electoral system for the next two elections, unless there is a further resolution or a poll of electors of the local authority.

Before 2001, local body elections were conducted on a first-past-the-post (FPP) basis. Pursuant to the 2001 Act, a number of local authorities use the STV system for their elections. The STV system allows voters to rank candidates in order of preference.

§3. Local Government Commission

351. The Commission comprises three members appointed by the Minister of Local Government, one of whom is elected Chairperson. Appointment is for a five-year term.[778] The role of the Commission is to provide information about local government and to promote good local government practice.[779] The Commission is to be treated as a Commission of Inquiry, with the authority to summon witnesses and the production of documents or consider any other matter useful to its investigation.[780]

777. Sections 58, 58A, and 58AA.
778. Local Government Act 2002, s. 33 and sch. 4.
779. Section 30.
780. Section 34.

Part IV. Citizenship and the Administration of Justice

Chapter 1. Rules Concerning Nationality and Relevance of Nationality

§1. Acquisition and Loss of Citizenship

352. New Zealand's citizenship law is found in the Citizenship Act 1977.[781] Historically, residents of New Zealand were British subjects. Following the British Nationality Act 1948 (UK), this status was altered. Self-governing Dominions were empowered to pass local citizenship laws, whilst retaining British subject rights.

Consequently, New Zealand enacted the British Nationality and New Zealand Citizenship Act 1948. This made New Zealand-born persons New Zealand citizens and British subjects. The Act was in force in New Zealand's component territories, as well as for Western Samoa, which at the time was a UN trust territory under New Zealand administration. British subjects born in Western Samoa before 1 January 1949 became New Zealand citizens.

353. The Citizenship Act 1977 was passed to provide an effective status for New Zealand citizenship. It repealed the British Nationality and New Zealand Citizenship Act 1948.

354. The Citizenship Act 1977 provides that every person born in New Zealand[782] after 1 January 1949 and before 1 January 2006 is a New Zealand citizen by birth.[783] A person born in New Zealand after 1 January 2006 is a New Zealand

781. There are also relevant provisions in the Citizenship (Western Samoa) Act 1982. The procedural component of the law is found in the Citizenship Regulations 2002 (SR 2002/73).

782. Section 2 of the Act defines New Zealand as including New Zealand, the Cook Islands, Niue, Tokelau and the Ross Dependency.

783. Section 6. Under the Citizenship Amendment Act (No. 2) 2001, persons deemed to be a child of a New Zealand citizen by s. 3 were extended to include a person who has been legally adopted by that citizen in Niue, Tokelau or the Cook Islands. A person born outside New Zealand is deemed to be a citizen if one of their parents is a citizen and they are working overseas for the public service of Niue, Tokelau or the Cook Islands. In terms of a grant of New Zealand citizenship (under s. 8 and 8A), the requirement that the applicant is entitled in terms of the Immigration Act to be in New Zealand indefinitely can be waived for applicants entitled to reside indefinitely in Niue, Tokelau or the Cook Islands.

citizen by birth if at the time of this person's birth at least one of the parents was a New Zealand citizen or was entitled to reside in New Zealand, Cook Islands, Niue or Tokelau indefinitely. This excludes diplomats' children and children of enemy aliens. Every person born outside New Zealand after 1 January 1978 to a parent who is a New Zealand citizen otherwise than by descent is a New Zealand citizen by descent.[784] Citizens by descent do not automatically transfer their citizenship status to their descendants.

The Act also provides for the grant of citizenship as of right to persons born outside New Zealand, before 1 January 1978, whose mother was a New Zealand citizen otherwise than by descent.[785]

355. Ordinary grants may be made to people of 18 years old or above who are of full capacity. The Minister must be satisfied that the applicant meets various requirements. The applicant must for example:

(i) have resided in New Zealand for the five years prior to the application;
(ii) by virtue of the Immigration Act 2009, be entitled to remain in New Zealand indefinitely;
(iii) be of good character;
(iv) understand the responsibilities and privileges of New Zealand citizenship;
(v) have sufficient knowledge of the English language;
(vi) intend to reside in New Zealand or to work abroad for an agency associated with New Zealand.

The Minister may waive the requirements as to length of residence or knowledge of English if the enforcement of these requirements would cause undue hardship to the applicant.[786]

356. Grants of citizenship may also be made in special cases.[787] This covers special grants to minors, to people whose parents were citizens by descent, and to people to whom because of particular circumstances of a humanitarian nature, a grant of citizenship would be in the public interest. It also covers grants of citizenship to people who would otherwise be stateless.

The ministerial grant of citizenship may be conditional on the taking of an oath of allegiance to the Sovereign or making an affirmation to similar effect.[788] The grant of citizenship is confirmed by a certificate from the Secretary for Internal Affairs.[789]

784. Section 7.
785. Section 10. This provision remedies the discrimination caused by the British Nationality and New Zealand Citizenship Act 1948 which provided that citizenship was acquired by birth on or after 1 Jan. 1949 outside New Zealand but only if that person's father was a New Zealand citizen otherwise than by descent: s. 7 of the 1948 Act.
786. Section 8.
787. Section 9.
788. Section 11.
789. Section 12.

357. Loss of citizenship can occur by renunciation.[790] A person who is 18 years old and of full capacity and who has citizenship of another country may renounce New Zealand citizenship although the Minister may decline to register the renunciation if the applicant is ordinarily resident in New Zealand or if New Zealand is at war. People over 18 years may also be deprived of citizenship if they acquire overseas citizenship and then act in a manner contrary to New Zealand interests, or who exercise the privileges of another citizenship contrary to New Zealand citizenship.[791] Deprivation of citizenship may also occur in the cases of citizens who have acquired citizenship by registration or naturalization under the 1948 Act or by grant under the 1977 Act or the Citizenship (Western Samoa) Act 1982, by fraudulent means.[792]

Prior to making deprivation orders, the Minister must notify the individuals concerned who have a right to apply within twenty days to have the matter reviewed by the High Court.[793]

358. The provisions of the Act are, in various forms, also in force in Tokelau, the Cook Islands and Niue.[794]

359. There is no prohibition on the holding of multiple citizenships.

§2. Privileges and Duties of New Zealand Citizenship

360. There are a limited number of benefits that derive from citizenship as opposed to residence; for example, foreign travel and the right to return to New Zealand on a New Zealand passport, and certain economic rights.[795] New Zealand citizens qualify for education rights such as subsidized fees, and scholarships. Some of these rights also extend to permanent residents of New Zealand. Permanent residents who are students qualify as 'domestic' students pursuant to the Education Act 1989, thereby entitling them to free primary and secondary education[796] and reduced fees for tertiary education.[797] Social welfare benefits and entitlements may generally be obtained by those who are ordinarily resident in New Zealand.[798]

In the electoral area both citizens and permanent residents are entitled to vote in general elections[799] although a person must be a New Zealand citizen before standing for Parliament.[800]

790. Section 15.
791. Section 16.
792. Section 17.
793. Section 19.
794. Section 29. Section 2 of the Act defines New Zealand to include the Cook Islands, Niue, Tokelau and the Ross Dependency. Both the Cook Islands and Niue specifically requested that the Acts be extended, pursuant to the request and consent provisions in their respective Constitutions.
795. Such as ownership of farm land. *See*, s. 16 of the Overseas Investment Act 2005.
796. Education Act 1989, ss 2 and 3.
797. Sections 2, 227 and 228.
798. Social Security Act 1964, ss 3 and 74A.
799. Electoral Act 1993, s. 74.
800. Section 47.

361. Some privileges are reserved solely for New Zealand citizens. Under the Passports Act 1992, New Zealand citizens are entitled as of right to a New Zealand passport[801] subject only to the requirements set out in the Act. Passports may be refused to New Zealand citizens who are under 16 years old and who do not have parental consent, or to citizens who are subject to arrest warrants, to bail or other orders of supervision, or who are required to surrender, or who already hold a passport.[802]

Under the Citizenship Act 1977, non-New Zealand citizens are able to acquire and dispose of real property as if they were New Zealand citizens. However, the provision specifically excludes ownership of a ship registered in New Zealand and will not qualify an alien to hold an office to which the alien would not be entitled, or entitle an alien to acquire property without any consents required under the Overseas Investment Act 2005 or per se entitle a person to the privileges of a New Zealand citizen.[803]

801. Section 3.
802. Section 4.
803. Section 23.

Chapter 2. Fundamental Rights and Liberties

§1. Legislative Background

362. Until 1990 New Zealand was without a written document containing a set of fundamental rights and freedoms. Instead rights as between the State and the individual, and between individuals were maintained as part of the common law tradition inherited from Great Britain and pursuant to statutes such as the Human Rights Act 1977. Parliament's power was kept in check principally by regular elections, by a politician's individual integrity, and through submissions made by the public on proposed legislation and considered by a Select Committee made up of members of both the Opposition and Government, and by judicial support of the rule of law.

Parliamentary officers such as the Ombudsman, the Auditor-General and the Commissioner for the Environment[804] also provided checks and balances on governmental power in different areas.

363. Inherent in this tradition is hundreds of years of common law development of civil liberties and human rights.[805] Generally, there is a common law right to do anything that is not expressly prohibited. Therefore, fundamental freedoms exist independently of being laid down in writing. The Magna Carta[806] and the English Bill of Rights[807] were attempts to legislate some rights – such as trial by peers, no tax without law, the right of a citizen to justice in the courts and the right not to be subject to cruel and unjust punishment. In the Imperial Laws Application Act 1988 New Zealand affirmed specified inherited laws, such as these, as part of the law of New Zealand.[808]

364. The judiciary in New Zealand has helped ensure that Parliament and the executive do not overstep their powers. However, parliamentary legislation is not

804. The Ombudsman and the Auditor-General are discussed in Part II, Ch. 6 above. The office of Commissioner for the Environment was established under the Environment Act 1986. The Commissioner is an officer of Parliament appointed by the Governor-General on recommendation of the House of Representatives for a five-year term: ss 4 and 6. The Commissioner may not be removed except on an address by the House on the grounds of disability, bankruptcy, neglect of duty or misconduct: s. 7. The office has functions under the Environment Act 1986 such as advising Parliament on legislation having environmental impact, and promoting environmental protection: s. 16. It also has responsibilities under other Acts such as the Resource Management Act 1991. The Commissioner has investigatory powers in regard to various environmental issues: s. 19. However, the office does not have executive authority but rather reports to Parliament and relies on adverse publicity generated by its recommendations.

805. For instance the right to be free from unreasonable search and seizure and the privilege against self-incrimination.

806. (1297) 25 Edw 1, Ch. 29.

807. (1688) 1 Will and Mar, Sess 2, Ch. 2.

808. Section 3 and sch. 1.

subject to judicial review. It is possible, therefore, that Parliament could enact legislation overriding the established common law freedoms and rights.[809]

365. New Zealand is a party to the key United Nations document, the Universal Declaration of Human Rights adopted by the United Nations on 10 December 1948. New Zealand made submissions on the draft document in response to the United Nations request in 1947 for member comments and was actively involved in the debate which culminated in the adoption of the Declaration.[810] Additionally, New Zealand has ratified the International Covenant on Civil and Political Rights and the International Covenant on Economic, Social and Political Rights.[811] In 1989, New Zealand acceded to the Optional Protocol to the International Covenant on Civil and Political Rights. The Optional Protocol allows individuals to petition their governments seeking protection on human rights matters and possible breaches of civil rights matters. Once local remedies are exhausted, the person is then able to take the complaint to the Human Rights Committee of the United Nations which will investigate the matter. In 1990, New Zealand also ratified the Second Optional Protocol to the Covenant on Civil and Political Rights, which concerned the abolition of the death penalty.

Examples of other United Nations instruments ratified by New Zealand are: the International Convention on the Elimination of all Forms of Racial Discrimination;[812] the International Convention on the Prevention and Punishment of the Crime of Genocide;[813] the International Convention on the Elimination of All Forms of Discrimination against Women;[814] the International Convention against Torture and other Cruel, Inhuman or Degrading Treatment or Punishment;[815] and the Convention on the Rights of the Child.[816]

366. The International Covenants which New Zealand has ratified are legally binding treaties, but they do not become law in New Zealand unless they are reflected in a statute. Legislation may already exist, or it may need to be amended or new legislation drafted to fulfil commitments to international obligations. Where provisions cannot be met, reservations must be made to the Covenants at the time of ratification.[817]

---

809. The Parliament occasionally allows subordinate legislation to override primary legislation. For example, the Canterbury Earthquake Response and Recovery Act 2010 (now repealed) allowed an Order in Council to grant exemption from, or modify, or extend any provision of any enactment: s. 6(4).
810. H. Fawthorpe, *Human Rights*, in *New Zealand as an International Citizen: Fifty Years of United Nations Membership* 97, 98 (Ministry of Foreign Affairs and Trade, 1995).
811. These documents were adopted by the United Nations in 1966. They came into force in 1976. New Zealand signed the documents in 1968 and ratified them in 1978.
812. New Zealand ratified this document in 1972.
813. New Zealand ratified this document in 1978.
814. New Zealand ratified this document in 1984.
815. New Zealand ratified this document in 1989.
816. New Zealand ratified this document in 1993.
817. For example, New Zealand has made reservations in respect of the International Covenant on Civil and Political Rights, the International Covenant on Economic, Social and Political Rights, and the International Convention on the Elimination of All Forms of Discrimination against Women.

367. The commitment to human rights resulted in the enactment of several key human rights statutes the Race Relations Act 1971[818] and the Human Rights Commission Act 1977,[819] (both of which are now consolidated in the Human Rights Act 1993) and the New Zealand Bill of Rights Act 1990.

§2. HUMAN RIGHTS ACT 1993

368. In 1977, New Zealand enacted the Human Rights Commission Act to establish a Human Rights Commission which would promote the advancement of human rights in New Zealand as required by the United Nations International Covenants on Human Rights.

369. The Act was consolidated in the Human Rights Act 1993. The Commission consists of a Chief Commissioner, a Race Relations Commissioner (formerly the Race Relations Conciliator), an Equal Employment Opportunities Commissioner, and no more than five other part-time commissioners.[820] The appointments are by the Governor-General on the recommendation of the Minister of Justice.[821]

The functions of the Chief Commissioner are set out in section 15. The functions of the Race Relations Commissioner are set out in section 16. The functions of the Equal Employment Opportunities Commissioner are set out in section 17.

Special meetings of the Commission can be called by the Race Relations Commissioner or, according to relevant provisions in the Crown Entities Act 2004, by the Chairperson (the Chief Commissioner) or any two Commissioners.[822]

370. Overall, the Commission has a wide brief to monitor and uphold the observance of international human rights in New Zealand in accordance with international standards. Its functions are comprehensively spelt out in the Act and include promotion, encouragement and education of human rights, inquiries into possible human rights infringements, reporting to the Prime Minister on human rights matters including the desirability of New Zealand becoming bound by any particular international instrument and the implication of proposed legislation on human rights. It also has functions in respect of examining current legislation for human rights compliance.[823]

371. The Act records numerous situations in which discrimination may occur. The key provision of the Act prohibits discrimination on the basis of sex, marital

818. To implement the International Convention on the Elimination of all Forms of Racial Discrimination.
819. To implement the various United Nations Covenants on Human Rights.
820. Section 8.
821. Section 11.
822. Section 10.
823. Section 5.

status, religious belief, ethical belief, colour, race, ethnic or national origin, disability, age, political opinion, employment status, family status and sexual orientation.[824] Special provisions provide for prevention of discrimination on a range of other matters including employment,[825] provision of housing and accommodation[826] and access to educational institutions.[827]

In addition it is unlawful to incite racial disharmony,[828] to commit sexual or racial harassment[829] or to victimize any person.[830] There are typically exceptions to every category, for example in the employment category the anti-discrimination provision is not applicable in respect of crews on ships and aircraft, work involving national security, or work performed outside New Zealand.[831]

There is also a reverse discrimination provision which excuses potential breaches of the Act where the action is done in good faith to assist persons who may need the assistance in order to achieve an equal standing in the community.[832]

372. The Act contains extensive provisions for complaints.

I. Office of the Human Rights Proceedings

373. The Office of the Human Rights Proceedings is part of the Human Rights Commission, and is headed by a Director of the Human Rights Proceedings.[833] The Director is appointed by the Governor-General on the recommendation of the Minister of Justice.[834]

II. Human Rights Review Tribunal

374. The chief function of the Tribunal is to hear proceedings brought under the Act.[835] Procedurally, sittings of the Tribunal are held at the determination of the Tribunal or its Chairperson.[836] Tribunal sittings are typically held in public.[837] The Tribunal may receive evidence and take evidence on oath, summon witnesses and has the power to commit for contempt.[838]

824. Section 21.
825. Section 22.
826. Section 53.
827. Section 57.
828. Section 61.
829. Sections 62–63.
830. Section 66.
831. Sections 24–26.
832. Section 73.
833. Section 20(1).
834. Section 20A(1).
835. Section 94.
836. Section 104.
837. Section 107.
838. Sections 106, 109, 110 and 114.

Persons entitled to be heard before the Tribunal are those who are parties to the proceedings or who satisfy the Tribunal that they have an interest in the proceedings which is greater than that of the general public.[839]

A number of remedies are available to the Tribunal once it has concluded that a defendant has committed a breach of the Act. These include declaring that the defendant has breached the provisions of the Act, making an order restraining the defendant from continuing or perpetrating the breach and awarding damages against the defendant.[840] Provision is given in the Act for appeal to the High Court against decisions of the Tribunal in certain instances, and from there appeals to the Court of Appeal against determinations of the High Court, on points of law.[841]

§3. New Zealand Bill of Rights Act 1990

375. This is a very important piece of legislation confirming New Zealand's commitment to human rights. Its purpose is to 'affirm New Zealand's commitment to the International Covenant on Civil and Political Rights'.[842]

376. In 1985, a White Paper[843] proposal for an entrenched Bill of Rights was published by the Minister of Justice. The proposal was rejected mainly because of its entrenched nature and the power the Bill would give the judiciary. In 1989, the proposal was reintroduced, but as an ordinary statute. The Bill was passed in 1990. The rights it protects are civil and political in nature, such as freedom of expression, religion and association; rights concerning the life and security of the person; non-discrimination and minority rights; and rights relating to search, arrest and detention.[844]

377. The Act is not supreme law and can therefore be amended or repealed by Parliament without special procedures. None of its provisions are entrenched. No enactments shall be held to be impliedly repealed merely because they are inconsistent with any provision of the New Zealand Bill of Rights Act.[845] The Act provides, however, that the rights and freedoms in the Bill of Rights 'may be subject only to such reasonable limits prescribed by law as can be demonstrably justified in a free and democratic society'.[846] It provides that wherever an enactment can be

839. Section 108.
840. Section 92I. An award of damages is covered by s. 92M–92O.
841. Sections 123–124.
842. Long title.
843. *A Bill of Rights for New Zealand: A White Paper*, 1985 AJHR A.6. *See also*, the Justice and Law Reform Committee, 'Interim Report of the Inquiry into the White Paper – A Bill of Rights for New Zealand', AJHR X(1986–1987): I.8A and the Justice and Law Reform Committee, *Final Report on a White Paper: A Bill of Rights for New Zealand* AJHR (1987–1990): I.8C.
844. Part 2 of the New Zealand Bill of Rights Act 1990. To date this is the most invoked part of the Act.
845. Section 4.
846. Section 5.

given a meaning consistent with the rights and freedoms contained in the Bill of Rights, that meaning must be preferred.[847]

378. The Act is applicable to the legislative, executive and judicial branches of the Government of New Zealand or to any person or body performing a public function, power or duty pursuant to law.[848]

379. The Bill of Rights has become an important expression of civil and political rights in New Zealand. In their treatment of the Bill of Rights, the courts have upheld the document as an important constitutional document, acknowledging that fundamental rights exist and are affirmed in the Act, but also exist independently of it. The courts have declared their intention to adopt a purposive approach and to treat the Bill as a living instrument – not to construe it narrowly and technically.[849] Rights are to be interpreted afresh and are not to be frozen in their common law status or their pre-Bill of Rights status.

380. Although the Act contains no provision for enforcement or remedies relating to the rights which it contains, the courts have actively sought to impose remedies. In *R v. Goodwin*[850] Richardson J held:[851] 'the Courts will affirmatively protect those fundamental rights and freedoms by recourse to appropriate remedies within their jurisdiction'.

Later in *Simpson v. Attorney-General (Baigent's Case)*[852] Casey J held:[853]

> I do not regard the absence of a remedies provision in the Act as an impediment to the Court's ability to 'develop the possibilities of judicial remedy' as envisaged in Article 3(b). The rights and freedoms affirmed are fundamental to a civilized society and justify a liberal purposive interpretation of the Act, even though it has not been constitutionally entrenched and has the same status as ordinary legislation. Its purpose being the affirmation of New Zealand's commitment to the Covenant (including Article 3(b)), it would be wrong to conclude that Parliament did not intend there to be any remedy for those whose rights have been infringed. Certainly section 6 provides that other enactments are to be given a meaning consistent with the Bill's rights and freedoms when that can be done; and section 7 requires the Attorney-General to draw the attention of the House to apparent inconsistencies in proposed legislation. It also helps to establish a legal climate in which the importance of those rights and freedoms will be stressed. But those provisions do little to vindicate the individual rights so strongly affirmed in the Act which is aimed at protecting and promoting them. I do not accept that Parliament intended it to be what most

847. Section 6.
848. Section 3.
849. *See,* for example *Flickinger v. Crown Colony of Hong Kong* [1991] 1 NZLR 439.
850. [1993] 2 NZLR 153.
851. At 191.
852. [1994] 3 NZLR 667.
853. At 691.

> would regard as no more than legislative window-dressing, of no practical consequence, in the absence of appropriate remedies for those whose rights and freedoms have been violated.

The Judge was referring to Article 2(3) of the International Covenant on Civil and Political Rights.

An example of the courts imposing remedies for specific breaches arises in respect of admissibility of evidence in criminal prosecutions. The courts will prima facie exclude evidence where there has been a breach of the Bill of Rights involved in obtaining that evidence. This occurred in *R v. Kirifi*[854] where the accused was not informed of his right to consult a lawyer at the correct moment pursuant to section 23 of the Bill of Rights; some evidence was therefore ruled inadmissible.

381. Rights of a cultural, social and economic nature are not protected under the Bill of Rights.

854. [1992] 2 NZLR 8.

Chapter 3. Constitutional Problems of Minorities

§1. History

382. The largest cultural grouping in New Zealand is the Europeans (Pakeha); the next largest is the Maori. A significant grouping also comprises Pacific Islanders.[855] New Zealand has been a monocultural society for most of the late nineteenth and twentieth centuries. Minority groups are largely expected to conform to European values and practices. Minority groups, predominantly Maori, but including Pacific Islanders, Chinese, Indians and other Europeans have had to operate within Anglo-Saxon oriented political, economic and education structures.

383. When the Europeans began settling in New Zealand Maori people had already been established for several centuries. They were organized in largely independent tribes with tightly run systems and structures:

> Maori society was both homogenous, with a shared belief system, culture and language, and varied, with strong tribal identity based on kinship. There was a recognised chiefly leadership, partly hereditary, partly ascribed by prowess in battle and ability to support kin.[856]

In 1835, some tribal chiefs signed a Declaration of Independence declaring the country to be independent. They designated themselves as the United Tribes of New Zealand. The document, 'The Declaration of Independence of New Zealand: He Wakaputanga o te Rangatiratanga o Nu Tireni' was signed at Waitangi in the Bay of Islands in October 1835. Under Article 1 of the document, sovereign power within the territories of the United Tribes was held to reside with the chiefs and tribal heads. Legislative authority could only be exercised by those who had the authority of the chiefs and were acting under the laws of the Confederation. The Confederation document asked the Sovereign of England to be the parent of the State and to protect its independence in return for the continued goodwill shown to British subjects and traders in New Zealand. The Confederation had limited success.[857]

384. Contemporary social and political factors provided the impetus for drafting a treaty to be signed by the Maori chiefs and representatives of the British Crown. The main signing took place on 6 February 1840 at Waitangi, a seaside village in the north of New Zealand, but many chiefs' signatures were collected after 6 February.[858]

---

855. The 2013 Census elicited the following responses as to ethnic identification: New Zealand European 74%; New Zealand Maori 14.9%; Asian 11.8%; Pacific Islanders 7.4% (*2013 Census Quick Stats about Culture and Identity* (Wellington: Statistics New Zealand, 2014). The Maori and Pacific Island populations both have Government Departments (Te Puni Kokiri, Ministry of Maori Development, and the Ministry of Pacific Island Affairs) which promote their interests and concerns.
856. Claudia Orange, *The Treaty of Waitangi* 7 (Allen and Unwin NZ Ltd, 1987).
857. *Ibid.* at 19–23.
858. Some tribes refused to sign the Treaty.

385. The treaty is set out in three articles which deal respectively with government, land and citizenship:[859]

> THE TREATY OF WAITANGI (TE TIRITI O WAITANGI) (THE TEXT IN ENGLISH)
>
> HER MAJESTY VICTORIA Queen of the United Kingdom of Great Britain and Ireland regarding with Her Royal Favour the Native Chiefs and Tribes of New Zealand and anxious to protect their just Rights and Property and to secure to them the enjoyment of Peace and Good Order has deemed it necessary in consequence of the great number of Her Majesty's Subjects who have already settled in New Zealand and the rapid extension of Emigration both from Europe and Australia which is still in progress to constitute and appoint a functionary properly authorised to treat with the Aborigines of New Zealand for the recognition of Her Majesty's Sovereign authority over the whole or any part of those islands – Her Majesty therefore being desirous to establish a settled form of Civil Government with a view to avert the evil consequences which must result from the absence of the necessary Laws and Institutions alike to the native population and to Her subjects has been graciously pleased to empower and to authorise me William Hobson a Captain in Her Majesty's Royal Navy Consul and Lieutenant Governor of such parts of New Zealand as may be or hereafter shall be ceded to her Majesty to invite the confederated and independent Chiefs of New Zealand to concur in the following Articles and Conditions.
>
> ARTICLE THE FIRST
>
> The Chiefs of the Confederation of the United Tribes of New Zealand and the separate and independent Chiefs who have not become members of the Confederation cede to Her Majesty the Queen of England absolutely and without reservation all the rights and powers of Sovereignty which the said Confederation or Individual Chiefs respectively exercise or possess, or may be supposed to exercise or to possess over their respective Territories as the sole Sovereigns thereof.
>
> ARTICLE THE SECOND
>
> Her Majesty the Queen of England confirms and guarantees to the Chiefs and Tribes of New Zealand and to the respective families and individuals thereof the full exclusive and undisturbed possession of their Lands and Estates Forests Fisheries and other properties which they may collectively or individually possess so long as it is their wish and desire to retain the same in their possession; but the Chiefs of the United Tribes and the individual Chiefs yield to Her Majesty the exclusive right of Preemption over such lands as may be agreed upon between the respective Proprietors and persons appointed by Her Majesty to treat with them in that behalf.
>
> ARTICLE THE THIRD

859. The provisions of the Treaty of Waitangi are set out in the First Schedule to the Treaty of Waitangi Act 1975.

In consideration thereof Her Majesty the Queen of England extends to the Natives of New Zealand Her royal protection and imparts to them all the Rights and Privileges of British Subjects.
W. HOBSON Lieutenant Governor.
Now therefore We the Chiefs of the Confederation of the United Tribes of New Zealand being assembled in Congress at Victoria in Waitangi and We the Separate and Independent Chiefs of New Zealand claiming authority over the Tribes and Territories which are specified after our respective names, having been made fully to understand the Provisions of the foregoing Treaty, accept and enter into the same in the full spirit and meaning thereof: in witness of which we have attached our signatures or marks at the places and the dates respectively specified.
Done at Waitangi this Sixth day of February in the year of Our Lord One thousand eight hundred and forty.

386. Problems have arisen in the interpretation of the Treaty as neither the Maori nor English versions are translations of the other. The discrepancies have fuelled debate over the precise effect of the Treaty of Waitangi for both Crown and Maori.

387. It must be noted that at the time the Treaty was signed, the Maori people were the majority and the Pakeha a distinct minority.[860] From a Maori perspective, by signing the Treaty they were affirming a need for the Pakeha to have a governor to control them. They also saw the Treaty as a covenant. Its promises and guarantees entailed a binding agreement, similar to God's covenant with the Israelite nation.[861] It was more than a mere contract that could be rescinded. Maori have continued to respect the Treaty, invoking its guarantees, on the whole unsuccessfully, until recently. However, on the Pakeha side, this solemn document had come, by the end of the nineteenth century, to be viewed as a matter of historical interest only.

388. In the nineteenth century one of the first cases of interest relating to the Treaty of Waitangi was *R v. Symonds*.[862] This case concerned competing claims to title to land: the claimant derived title from Maori, and had a certificate from the Governor waiving the Crown's right to acquire the land. The defendant had title by grant from the Crown. The case expounded the common law doctrine of aboriginal title or customary title. The doctrine held that indigenous people had status and rights in respect of the occupancy and use of the land. According to the doctrine

860. It is difficult to make an exact comparison. The *New Zealand Official 1990 Yearbook* (94th ed., Department of Statistics 1990) comments that as at 1840 the Maori population was between 100,000 and 125,000 and the European population little more than 1,000 throughout the whole country. By 1845, however, about 9,000 settlers had been brought to New Zealand by the New Zealand company: *see,* 27–29. Claudia Orange, *The Treaty of Waitangi* estimates that there were around 2000 permanent settlers in 1839, 1,400 in the North Island and 600 in the South (although many transients passed through). She comments that European estimates of the Maori population in 1840 ranged from 90,000 to 200,000: *see,* 6–7.

861. Orange, 57.

862. (1847) NZPCC 387. *See also, Te Runanganui o Te Ika Whenua Inc. Society v. Attorney-General* [1994] 2 NZLR 20 which reiterated the concept of aboriginal title.

such rights continue until expressly extinguished by the Crown making a grant of the land. Clearly these rights existed independently of the Treaty of Waitangi, though the Treaty can be seen to be affirming the principle of aboriginal title.

The Court commented:[863]

> in solemnly guaranteeing the Native title, and in securing what is called the Queen's pre-emptive right, the Treaty of Waitingi, confirmed by the Charter of the Colony, does not assert either in doctrine or practice anything new and unsettled.

389. Over the years, however, the status of the Treaty was eroded. Partly this can be seen as a result of the changing New Zealand society. The Government sought to encourage settlement; policies of assimilation and land acquisition were actively pursued by successive Governments. This eventually began to deny Maori, to a large extent, their identity, values. cultural distinctiveness, as well as of their taonga[864] which included the land, language and rights to customary fishing.

390. The ultimate expression of the Treaty's lack of value came in *Wi Parata v. Bishop of Wellington.*[865] This case concerned a tribe which in 1848 entered into an oral agreement with the Bishop of Wellington to endow land for the purposes of a school. In 1850, without tribal consent a Crown grant was issued to the Bishop of Wellington. The plaintiffs sought to have the Crown grant declared void. The Court refused to do this holding that any agreement between the tribe and the Bishop was a legal nullity since the right to extinguish native title rested only with the Crown and could not be called into question by the Court. The Court reasoned that, in the absence of civilized government in New Zealand, the Crown was compelled to assume the rights and duties which the uncivilized occupants could not assume. In reference to the Treaty of Waitangi the Court held:[866]

> On the cession of territory by one civilised power to another, the rights of private property are invariably respected, and the old law of the country is administered, to such an extent as may be necessary, by the Courts of the new sovereign … But in the case of primitive barbarians, the supreme executive government must acquit itself, as best it may, of its obligation to respect native property rights, and of necessity must be the sole arbiter of its own justice. Its acts in this particular case cannot be examined or called in question by any tribunal, because there exist no known principles whereon a regular adjudication can be based. …
>
> The existence of the pact known as the 'Treaty of Waitangi' entered into by Captain Hobson on the part of Her Majesty with certain natives at the Bay of Islands, and adhered to by some other natives of the Northern Island, is

863. Page 390. Note also s. 84 of the Native Land Act 1909: 'Save so far as otherwise expressly provided in any other Act the native customary title to land shall not be available or enforceable as against His Majesty the King by any proceedings in any Court or in any other manner.'
864. Treasures or things of value. *See*, Angelo, *Taonga and Personality*, VUWLR 26 (1996).
865. (1877) 3 NZ Jur (NS) 72.
866. Page 78.

perfectly consistent with what has been stated. So far indeed as that instrument purported to cede sovereignty – a matter with which we are not here directly concerned – it must be regarded as a simple nullity. No body politic existed capable of making cession of sovereignty, nor could the thing itself exist. So far as the proprietary rights of the natives are concerned, the so-called treaty merely affirms the rights and obligations which jure gentium, vested in and devolved upon the Crown under the circumstances of the case.

391. A third significant case occurred in 1941. In *Hoani Te Heu Heu Tukino v. Aotea District Maori Land Board*[867] the Privy Council confirmed the validity of the Treaty but held that rights conferred by a treaty of cession could not be enforced in court except to the extent that they were also statutorily recognized.

392. The establishment of the Waitangi Tribunal under the Treaty of Waitangi Act 1975 went some way towards redressing the imbalance between the cultures and was the first significant step in a chain of events which saw the Treaty accorded a major constitutional status. The Tribunal was set up to hear claims by Maori that Crown action was prejudicial to them and inconsistent with the principles of the Treaty of Waitangi.[868]

In addition, in recent years there have been several cases on the Treaty which have confirmed that the Treaty of Waitangi is an important founding constitutional document.

§2. Recent Treaty Jurisprudence

I. Maori Fishing Rights

393. In 1986, the first modern Treaty case was heard. *Te Weehi v. Regional Fisheries Officer*[869] concerned Maori fishing rights. Section 88(2) of the Fisheries Act 1983 stated that nothing in the Act affected any Maori fishing rights. The Court held that if the appellant was exercising a customary Maori fishing right, then the provisions of the Act which included details on the right to take fish did not apply to the appellant.

In 1988, the Waitangi Tribunal issued a report[870] and, drawing on *Te Weehi*, found that Maori did have commercial fishing rights and that the Government's Fisheries Quota Management System was in conflict with the Treaty of Waitangi. The quota system had revolutionized the fishing industry in New Zealand. It provided for the allocation of quotas to commercial fishing ventures. Quotas were to become transferable property rights. However, Maori fishing rights – neither commercial nor traditional – were taken into account. As a result many Maori objected to the system and this led to further litigation. The enactment of the Maori Fisheries Act 1989,

867. [1941] AC 308.
868. *See,* section on Waitangi Tribunal (paras 262–266 above) and its Reports.
869. [1986] 1 NZLR 680.
870. *Report of the Waitangi Tribunal on the Muriwhenua Fishing Claim* (1988) Wai 22.

retaining section 88(2) and providing for the transfer by the Crown to the Maori Fisheries Commission of 10% of the fishing quota, went only part of the way towards allaying Maori grievances.

In 1990, the first major fisheries decision was reported. In *Te Runanga o Muriwhenua Inc. v. Attorney-General,*[871] the Court of Appeal affirmed a High Court decision which found that before 1840 Maori had a highly developed fishery system which had survived the Treaty of Waitangi. The Court indicated that in some instances a fiduciary duty may rest on the Crown in respect of its obligations to Maori.

In 1992, Maori negotiators and the Crown reached a settlement. The essence of the agreement was that the Crown would finance Maori tribes in forming a joint venture to buy over 23% of the total fishing quota, and 20% of new quota. NZD 150 million was to be paid by the Crown to the Maori Fisheries Commission to develop the Maori fishing industry. Consequently Maori fishing claims would be regarded as settled, and claims under aboriginal title would be extinguished. The Deed of Settlement was signed on 23 September 1992 and the terms of the Agreement were implemented in the Treaty of Waitangi (Fisheries Claims) Settlement Act 1992.[872] The Agreement did not have the support of all Maori.[873] Several tribes which had not signed brought court proceedings challenging the Deed.

The case of *Te Runanga O Wharekauri Rekohu Inc. v. Attorney-General*[874] represented the culmination of Maori fishing matters. Those Maori opposed to the deal argued that it could not bind those who had not signed it. This was held to be immaterial since it was never intended to bind those who had not signed it. The Court held that there was 'an established principle of non-interference by the Courts in Parliamentary proceedings'.[875] It stated as follows:[876]

> Parliament is free to enact legislation on the lines envisaged in the deed or otherwise. Whether or not it would be wise to do so and whether there is a sufficient 'mandate' for any such legislation are political questions for political judgment. The Court is not concerned with such questions. Nor are we concerned with whether more direct steps should be taken at the present stage to ensure that Maori participate actively in the fishing industry in addition to such participation as already occurs through leasing of quota and employment. No issue under the New Zealand Bill of Rights Act 1990 arises now.
>
> Should any legislation be enacted in this field, there could be little point in bringing the matter again before the Courts until at least some years of experience have been gained, and perhaps not even then. No more than Parliament

871. [1990] 2 NZLR 641.
872. The legislation encompassed traditional Maori fishing rights: s. 10. The former consultative method of regulating tribal fisheries was replaced by a centralized bureaucracy to which Maori have less input.
873. A Waitangi Tribunal Report (*The Fisheries Settlement Report* (1992) Wai 307) had also expressed some doubts.
874. [1993] 2 NZLR 301.
875. Page 307.
876. Page 309.

itself can we bind our successors. All that can be said now is that a responsible and major step forward has been taken.

On the Treaty of Waitangi, the Court stated as follows:[877]

> The deed does not of course purport to repeal the Treaty of Waitangi. Clause 1.3 says as much, virtually expressly. Moreover a nation cannot cast adrift from its own foundations. The Treaty stands. Parliament is free, if it thinks fit, to repeal section 88(2) of the Fisheries Act and to make other legislative changes envisaged in the deed. Parliament was free to do so before the deed and remains free to do so afterwards. Whatever constitutional or fiduciary significance the Treaty may have of its own force, or as a result of past or present statutory recognition, could only remain.

II. Ownership of Maori Land and Government Privatization

394. During the 1980s considerable restructuring took place. Government pursued policies of privatization and sale of State assets. Many public sector bodies were turned into State-owned enterprises which could later be privatized. The State-Owned Enterprises Act 1986 provided that:[878]

> Nothing in this Act shall permit the Crown to act in a manner that is inconsistent with the principles of the Treaty of Waitangi.

In *New Zealand Maori Council v. Attorney-General*[879] the Maori Council sought to prevent disposal of assets which could be subject to decisions of the Waitangi Tribunal. The Court found that the principles and spirit of the Treaty rather than the literal words are the most important factors in determining the rights and guarantees the Treaty accords Maori today. More specifically the principles of the Treaty are: partnership between the races; that the Crown should act reasonably and in good faith and consistently with the principles of the Treaty; and according to Sir Robin Cooke, then President of the Court of Appeal, to actively protect 'Maori people in the use of their lands and waters to the fullest extent practicable'.[880] In return the Maori had undertaken to accept and to cooperate in Government. However, Treaty rights can still only be enforced insofar as the Treaty has been incorporated into statute.[881]

After this case the Treaty of Waitangi (State Enterprises) Act 1988 was enacted. This Act provided that the subjection of an asset to claims under the Treaty of Waitangi Act 1975 would not prevent its transferability to a State enterprise or by that

877. Pages 308–309.
878. Section 9.
879. [1987]1 NZLR 641.
880. Page 664.
881. This position was affirmed in *New Zealand Maori Council v. Attorney-General* [1992] 2 NZLR 576.

enterprise to any other person. However, where the Waitangi Tribunal subsequently recommended that such land be returned to Maori ownership then the land would be resumed by the Crown and transferred into Maori ownership.[882]

This case is the most significant of the recent case law. Commenting on the decision in the case Sir Robin Cooke stated as follows:[883]

> To the President of the day it was gratifying and strengthening that our court was of the calibre where five independently-minded judges, not necessarily usually of the same mind in issues touching the relationship of the legislative and administrative arms of government and the courts, were able to reach the same conclusion. With naturally varying emphases and language, the judgments unite in defining Treaty principles in phrases such as partnership, fiduciary duty, active protection, full spirit, the honour of the Crown, fair and reasonable recompense for wrong, fundamental concepts, and satisfactory recompense. Of course these are generalizations, as was the Treaty itself.

395. In 2003, the Court of Appeal in *Ngati Apa v. Attorney-General*[884] had to determine the legal status of foreshore or seabed and waters. The High Court had held that land below low water mark was beneficially owned by the Crown and that land below low water mark could not be Maori customary land. The Court of Appeal found that the Crown did not acquire property in these areas when it acquired sovereignty over New Zealand, and that transfer of sovereignty did not affect customary title which was preserved by common law until extinguished by statute.[885]

III. Treaty Implementation

396. Ministers of the Crown must specify whether Bills which they are proposing to introduce comply with Treaty principles. Since 1986, any legislation referred to the Cabinet at policy approval stage should draw attention to any implications for the Treaty of Waitangi. Additionally Maori should be consulted as to the application of the Treaty in certain areas.

The legislation itself falls into various categories: some legislation states that regard must be had to the Treaty of Waitangi; other legislation requires compliance

---

882. Treaty of Waitangi (State Enterprises) Act 1988, s. 10 inserting new s. 27–27D into the State-Owned Enterprises Act 1986.

883. Rt Hon Sir Robin Cooke, 'The Challenge of Treaty of Waitangi Jurisprudence', 2 *Waikato LR* 1, at 6 (1994).

884. *Ngati Apa v. Attorney-General* [2003] 3 NZLR 643.

885. This decision resulted in a commitment by the government to legislate to vest the seabed and foreshore in the Crown. The proposal was highly controversial. The Waitangi Tribunal's report on the Crown's Foreshore and Seabed Policy (Wai 1071, 2004) found the proposal to be in breach of Arts 2 and 3 of the Treaty of Waitangi. The United Nations Committee on the Elimination of Racial Discrimination criticized the Act in its decision released in 2005 (CERD/C/66/NZL/ Dec.1) following a petition to the UN from the Treaty Tribes coalition. In September 2010 the government introduced the Marine and Coastal Area (Takutai Moana) Bill 2010, was passed in March 2011 and repealed the Foreshore and Seabed Act 2004.

with the principles of the Treaty. Some statutes are based on the Treaty and do not mention the Treaty at all. The Treaty is also appended to the Treaty of Waitangi Act 1975 but that does not incorporate the Treaty into municipal law. Despite all the developments the Treaty is not entrenched, and it is not yet a justiciable instrument.[886]

886. Joseph, 71.

Chapter 4. Judicial Control of Administrative Action

397. Judicial review of administrative action in New Zealand is controlled both by statutory provisions and common law rules. The courts' ability to review administrative action has grown considerably in the past fifty years, such that it now extends to every organization of major significance in the country's social structure.

398. The grounds for review are many and varied.[887] In summary, a decision may be challenged on one of three grounds:

Illegality.

The decision may be challenged on the grounds that it is illegal. This incorporates a number of heads:

- The decision is made for an improper purpose; that is, one that is outside the purpose or spirit of the Act.
- The purpose does not take into account certain relevant matters.
- The decision takes into account irrelevant matters.
- The decision is influenced by error in the facts.
- The decision-maker has applied a predetermined general policy which has failed to take account of the merits of the particular case.
- The decision-maker has acted under dictation from someone else.
- The decision-maker has acted under an invalid delegation of the power.

Unreasonableness.

The decision should not be so unreasonable that no sensible person could have reached it.

Natural justice/unfairness.

- This comes down to two principles of natural justice – the right to a fair hearing (*audi alterem partem*) and the rule against bias (*nemo judex in causa sua*). Both of these principles infer that the person subject to the decision has the right to be treated fairly.
- Right to a fair hearing: what this will involve will vary with the circumstances of each case. It may involve the duty to give an oral hearing, to give notice of any proposed findings, to give notice of allegations against the person, to give the person reasonable time to prepare their case or to disclose the relevant material.
- Rule against bias: this has two limbs. It may entail potential conflicts of interest on the basis of financial interest in the outcome of the decision, or it may be evinced by some other types of potential bias such as relationship with the party or animosity against, or friendship towards, the party. The legal test is to show a reasonable likelihood or a reasonable suspicion of bias.

887. The grounds have been categorized as illegality, irrationality and procedural impropriety: *Council of Civil Service Unions v. Minister for the Civil Service* [1985] AC 374, 410.

399. In practice, therefore, review action may lie where an authority does not act in accordance with law, or does not act fairly and reasonably. Such broad statements are translated into reality, for example, when an authority acts where it has no authority to act, where the wrong procedure was followed in the action,[888] where errors were made in the decision-making process,[889] or where the action went beyond the power which the actor had been granted.

400. To initiate a review, a plaintiff must have *locus standi*. Formerly, it was believed that sufficient standing meant a contractual relationship between plaintiff and reviewed organization, or alternatively, that the plaintiff's legal or property rights were affected. However, New Zealand authority now states that any person for whose benefit an organization exists may seek review of the organization's actions.[890]

401. The statute governing judicial review is the Judicature Amendment Act 1972. This Act creates a statutory entitlement to judicial review and regulates proceedings against persons and bodies exercising statutory powers. The Act sought to consolidate the prerogative writs of England into one action of review, and to provide a system of judicial review of administrative actions of the Crown against whom it was previously difficult to get prerogative writ remedies. The system exists in addition to the common law remedies, but is undoubtedly a simpler procedure.

The Act provides:[891]

> On an application by motion which may be called an application for review, the High Court may, notwithstanding any right of appeal possessed by the applicant in relation to the subject-matter of the application, by order grant, in relation to the exercise, refusal to exercise, or proposed or purported exercise by any person of a statutory power, any relief that the applicant would be entitled to, in any one or more of the proceedings for a writ or order of or in the nature of mandamus, prohibition or certiorari or for a declaration or injunction, against that person in any such proceedings.

A statutory power is:[892]

> a power or right conferred by or under any Act or by or under the constitution or other instrument of incorporation, rules, or bylaws of any body corporate –

888. For example, the action was contrary to the principles of natural justice.
889. For example, mistakes of fact or law, unreasonable decisions.
890. *Finnigan v. New Zealand Rugby Football Union* [1985] 2 NZLR 159.
891. Section 4(1).
892. Section 3. A statutory power of decision is also defined in the Act: 'a power or right conferred by or under any Act, or by or under the constitution or other instrument of incorporation, rules, or bylaws of any body corporate, to make a decision deciding or prescribing or affecting – (a) the rights, powers, privileges, immunities, duties or liabilities of any person; or (b) the eligibility of any person to receive, or to continue to receive, a benefit or licence, whether he is legally entitled to it or not'.

(a) To make any regulation, rule, bylaw, or order, or to give any notice or direction having force as subordinate legislation; or
(b) To exercise a statutory power of decision; or
(c) To require any person to do or refrain from doing any act or thing that, but for such requirement, he would not be required by law to do or refrain from doing; or
(d) To do any act or thing that would, but for such power or right, be a breach of the legal rights of any person; or
(e) To make any investigation or inquiry into the rights, powers, privileges, immunities, duties, or liabilities of any person.

402. When the Judicature Amendment Act 1972 was enacted, the grounds for review were believed to be limited to the wielding of statutory powers, but in 1977[893] the definition of statutory power was widened to include review of actions of incorporated bodies acting under their various instruments of incorporation, and not pursuant to a statute.

403. Under the Judicature Amendment Act 1972 the court is granted power to issue interim orders at the request of any party to the action. Such an order may prohibit any further action under the statutory power, prohibit court proceedings or declare a license to continue in force. Orders may continue in force until the application is fully heard, or as the court otherwise directs.[894] The Act also grants some flexibility of procedure to enable the judge to determine a review application expeditiously. Thus, a judge may call a conference between parties or counsel to determine issues, or require discovery of documents.[895]

404. The making of subordinate legislation is the exercise of a statutory power, and is specified as an item reviewable under the Judicature Amendment Act 1972. However, some of the grounds for reviewing subordinate legislation are arguably different from the grounds for reviewing other action. The most obvious ground is that the legislation made is beyond the scope of the power conferred by statute for making regulations. Similarly, subsidiary legislation may be challenged on the basis that there was no power to make it.

893. Judicature Amendment Act 1977.
894. Judicature Amendment Act 1972, s. 8.
895. Section 10.

Chapter 5. Legal Position of Aliens

§1. General

405. In times of peace the main concerns are with immigration and residence, and they are dealt with by statute. The rules relating to aliens impose some restrictions on aliens, particularly of a procedural nature in times of war. For the purposes of the Citizenship Act 1977 an alien is regarded as a person who is not a New Zealand citizen, a Commonwealth citizen (British subject), a British protected citizen or an Irish citizen.[896] Aliens therefore are both those with a recognized nationality and those who are stateless.[897]

406. Various provisions recognize New Zealand's obligations under international conventions. Under the Convention relating to the Status of Refugees, identity documents must be issued to refugees[898] in the territory who do not have travel documents, or refugees lawfully in the territory who wish to travel outside it.[899]

The Passports Act 1992 provides that certificates of identity may be issued to non-New Zealand citizens if they are unable to obtain a travel document in their own country. The document is neither a passport nor an emergency travel document, but it establishes identity and allows entry into, and exit from countries.[900]

Part 5 of the Immigration Act 2009 deals with refugee and protection status determinations. The purpose of this Part is to:[901]

> provide a statutory basis for the system by which New Zealand:
>
> (a) determines to whom it has obligations under the United Nations Convention Relating to the Status of Refugees and the Protocol Relating to the Status of Refugees; and
>
> (b) codifies certain obligations, and determines to whom it has these obligations, under:
>
> (i) the Convention against Torture and Other Cruel, Inhuman or Degrading Treatment or Punishment;
>
> (ii) the International Covenant on Civil and Political Rights.

---

896. Citizenship Act 1977, s. 2.

897. A stateless person is regarded as a person who is not a national of any State under the operation of its law. Convention relating to the Status of Stateless Persons 1954 (New York, 28/9/54: TS 41 of 1960; Cmnd 1098) Art. 1.

898. A refugee is a person who is outside the country of nationality (or has no nationality, but has been residing somewhere) and who because of fear on the basis of religious, racial or other reasons is unwilling to return to it: Convention relating to the Status of Refugees 1951 (Geneva, 28/7/51: TS 39 of 1954; NZTS (1961) No. 2; Cmnd 9171) Art. 1A(2).

899. Articles 27 and 28.

900. Passports Act 1992, ss 2 and 16.

901. Section 124.

Claims are to be determined by a refugee and protection officer.[902] Appeals to the Immigration and Protection Tribunal are possible.[903] The Citizenship Act 1977 has a special provision for the Minister of Internal Affairs to grant citizenship to a person who would otherwise be stateless.[904]

407. The position of people who are not New Zealanders, but who are in New Zealand is, for the most part, governed by the Immigration Act 2009.

408. The Act sets out various categories of eligibility for being in New Zealand. New Zealand citizens are guaranteed the right to be in New Zealand at any time.[905] Other people may travel to New Zealand if they hold a visa granted under the Act and comply with the conditions of the visa, or if a visa waiver applies to them.[906] They may be in New Zealand only if they hold a visa and have been granted entry permission.[907]

Holders of residence visas are entitled to dwell in the country indefinitely and they may undertake any employment or any course of study or training.[908] They enjoy most of the privileges of New Zealand citizens, are able to vote and receive social welfare benefits.

The decision to allow or decline the grant of a visa or entry permission rests with the Minister of Immigration or an immigration officer.[909] Every visa other than a permanent residence visa can be subject to conditions as prescribed by the Act.[910]

§2. Categories of Visa

409. There are essentially three classes of visa:[911]

(a) *Residence visas.* This includes permanent residence visas and residence visas.
(b) *Temporary entry class visas.* This includes temporary visas, limited visas and interim visas.
(c) *Transit visas.*

§3. Appeals

410. Appeals may be made to the Immigration and Protection Tribunal against refusals to grant a residence class visas, matters concerning recognition as a refugee

902. Section 127.
903. Sections 194 and 217.
904. Section 9(1)(d).
905. Section 13.
906. Section 14(1)(a).
907. Section 14(1)(b).
908. Sections 73 and 74.
909. Section 26.
910. Section 49.
911. Section 70.

or protected person, or liability for deportation.[912] Judicial review and appeals to the High Court and the Court of Appeal on a point of law by leave are also available.[913]

§4. Revocation of Permits

411. Residence permits may be revoked by an immigration officer on the grounds of administrative error, and by the Minister on the grounds of administrative error, where the permit was procured by fraud, or for failure to meet conditions placed on the permit.[914]

§5. Exemptions

412. Under the Immigration Act 1987, certain classes of people were exempt from the need to hold permits.[915] Under the Immigration Act 2009, these people are deemed to be holders of a temporary visa or resident visa.[916] These people include the crew, and some passengers, on board ships and aircraft which are in transit. Members of the armed forces of another country who are in New Zealand with the New Zealand Government's permission are also considered exempt, as are persons in the Ross Dependency associated with scientific programmes under the auspices of a contracting party to the Antarctic Treaty. Exemption is also given to any person entitled to immunity from jurisdiction by reason of the Diplomatic Privileges and Immunities Act 1968 or the Consular Privileges and Immunities Act 1971.

§6. Deportation Orders and Excluded Persons

413. A person is liable to be deported from New Zealand under certain conditions; for example, if this person is unlawfully in New Zealand, if the visa has been granted in error, if the visa is held under a false identity, if a residence class visa or citizenship is obtained by fraud or forgery, or if visa conditions are breached.[917]

There is a right of appeal to the Immigration and Protection Tribunal against liability for deportation.[918]

The Act also prescribes that certain convicted or deported persons are not eligible for visa entry permission to enter or be in New Zealand.[919] Furthermore, if the Minister has reason to believe that a person is likely to commit an offence in

912. Section 217.
913. Sections 245–247.
914. Section 432, preserving the effect of the Immigration Act 1987, relevant sections are ss 19 and 20.
915. Immigration Act 1987, s. 11.
916. Section 417.
917. Part 6.
918. Section 217.
919. *See,* s. 15.

New Zealand that is punishable by imprisonment, is or is likely to be a threat or risk to security, public order or to the public interest, or is a member of a terrorist entity designated under the Terrorism Suppression Act 2002, that person is not eligible for a visa, entry permission or visa waiver.[920]

920. Section 16.

Part V. Specific Problems

Chapter 1. War, Treaty and Foreign Affairs Powers

§1. War

414. The power to declare war and peace rests with the Sovereign acting in accordance with the advice of the Government.[921]

§2. Treaties

415. The New Zealand Government has the power to enter into treaties.[922] All multilateral treaties and 'major' bilateral treaties of particular significance must be presented to the House of Representatives for examination by the Foreign Affairs, Defence and Trade Select Committee before binding treaty action is taken.[923] However, in order to implement a treaty nationally, legislation is required. Many treaties operate without the need for legislation. In other cases the New Zealand law may not be in compliance with the proposed treaty legislation and amendments to legislation are then required unless reservations have been entered in respect of parts of the treaty.

Effect can be given to treaty obligations by incorporating provisions into existing law or specifically giving the treaty obligations the force of law.

New Zealand courts will as far as practicable interpret statutes in accordance with treaty obligations, particularly where the treaties are recognized as authoritatively stating the international law position.

---

921. Between 1899 and 1902 New Zealand sent a contingent to the South African or Boer War. Approximately 110,000 people went to the First World War in 1914 and 17,000 died in action. In 1939, 140,000 went to the Second World War and about 12,000 were killed in action. New Zealand also sent troops to the Korea War in 1950; to the Malaysia War in 1948 and to the Vietnam War in 1964 and in recent times to the Gulf, Falklands, Iraq and Afghanistan Wars. From 1845, men were liable for defence duties within their areas. This remained the case until about 1872 when the New Zealand wars eased. After that defence forces were compiled using volunteers only. In 1909, the Defence Act provided for European males under 25 to undergo military training. In 1916, and 1917 conscription was introduced for males between 17 and 60. Compulsory military training was phased out in 1930. Conscription was again introduced from June 1940 when men between 18 and 46 became liable to go to war. In 1949, the Compulsory National Service Act was passed. This required all 18 years old males to complete fourteen weeks of military training, then give three years part-time service and six years in reserve. That was abolished in 1958. Compulsory military training again existed between 1962 and 1972.

922. New Zealand Law Commission Report, *New Zealand Guide to International Law and Its Sources* (NZLC R 34, 1996, Wellington).

923. Standing Order 397; Cabinet Manual 2008, 7.118.

Because of the constitutional relations between New Zealand and Niue, the Cook Islands and Tokelau, the four jurisdictions have usually moved together in treaty matters. However, since 10 November 1988, no treaty signed by New Zealand will extend to the Cook Islands or Niue unless it is expressly signed on behalf of the Cook Islands or Niue.[924] By agreement, New Zealand will not extend treaties to Tokelau without first having consulted Tokelau.[925]

§3. Foreign Affairs

416. For about 100 years after the Treaty of Waitangi was signed, New Zealand had little in the way of foreign affairs because it relied on Great Britain for protection from military threats and as a market for produce. An overseas post was established in London in 1871, in Australia in 1906, in the USA in 1935, and later in Canada. Diplomatic posts were created in Russia in 1944 and in Japan in 1952. From 1950 onwards posts have been established throughout Asia, the European Continent, Latin America, the Middle East, Africa and the Pacific.

In 1943, the Department of External Affairs was established. That Department, now known as the Ministry of Foreign Affairs and Trade,[926] has the responsibility for advising and formulating policy for the New Zealand Government on international affairs. It is responsible for the administration of all overseas diplomatic posts. The Ministry is responsible for the administration of Tokelau.

§4. International Organizations Membership

417. New Zealand was a founding member of the United Nations and has actively participated in various aspects of that body such as contributing personnel and money to the peace-keeping and humanitarian role of the United Nations.

In addition New Zealand is also a member of a number of other international organizations such as the following:

- World Bank.
- Asian Development Bank.
- Organisation for Economic Cooperation and Development.
- International Whaling Commission.
- The Commonwealth.

924. *See,* the Declaration setting out the position of the Cook Islands and Niue with respect to New Zealand Treaty actions, dated 10 Nov. 1988 (New Zealand Declaration to the Secretary-General of the United Nations of 10 Nov. 1988, circulated as UNGA LE 222 New Zealand).
925. 'Joint Statement of the Principles of Partnership between New Zealand and Tokelau' (signed by the Ulu o Tokelau on behalf of Tokelau and the Associate Minister for Pacific Island Affairs on behalf of New Zealand, 21 November 2003), principle 10.
926. The Act governing the Ministry is the Foreign Affairs Act 1988.

Chapter 2. Taxation and Spending Power

418. The spending power is covered in an earlier part of this document.[927] The taxation regime comprises a number of statutes on taxation. The Tax Administration Act 1994 contains the administrative provisions regulating New Zealand's taxation regime.

§1. Taxation Regime

I. Personal Income Tax

419. New Zealand residents are liable to pay tax on all income derived in New Zealand and from overseas. Non-residents are liable to pay tax on income with a New Zealand source.

Personal income tax is levied under the Income Tax Act 2007 on most forms of income. Tax is levied either at source for salaries and wage earners or by provisional tax, payable in instalments throughout the year, for business and professional incomes. All taxpayers may deduct rebates from income. Rebates include income under a certain figure and donations. Provisional taxpayers may deduct some business expenses, incurred in producing the income.

II. Tax on Interest and Dividends

420. Resident withholding tax is deducted from interest and dividends at source.[928]

III. Fringe Benefit Tax

421. This is payable by an employer on an annual or quarterly basis. It is a tax on the value of fringe benefits provided by an employer to an employee, for example the use of a motor vehicle or a low interest loan.[929]

IV. Company Tax

422. Tax is levied under the Income Tax Act 2007. Companies are taxed differently from individuals.

927. *See above*, Part II, Ch. 3.
928. There are limited exemptions for resident withholding tax. *See*, s. 32E of the Tax Administration Act 1994.
929. *See*, s. CX 2–CX 38 of the Income Tax Act 2007.

V. Goods and Services Tax

423. The Goods and Services Tax (GST) is levied under the Goods and Services Tax Act 1985. A charge of 15% is levied on supplies provided in New Zealand by a registered person produced in the course of a taxable activity.

Any person supplying over NZD 60,000 worth of services in twelve months must register for GST though they may not need to register if the turnover in the following twelve months is unlikely to exceed NZD 60,000.[930]

Registered persons charge GST to their customers and account for it to the Inland Revenue Department. In turn registered persons who pay GST on purchases and expenses may later claim it back.

Some activities such as wages are not included as taxable activities.[931] Some activities are exempt,[932] for example financial services, and some are zero-rated[933] (such as products which are being exported).

VI. Accident Compensation Levy

424. Under the Accident Compensation Act 2001 an Accident Compensation Levy is collected for the Accident Compensation Corporation. It comprises:

(a) an earner premium which all employees and self-employed people must pay; employees have the sum deducted from their salaries or wages and the self-employed have to pay a Corporation calculated premium; and
(b) the employer premium which is paid by employers for their employees; the self-employed must pay the levy by the date specified for payment by the Corporation.[934]

The earner premium goes towards the cost of non-work-related injuries and the employer premium to work-related injuries.

§2. Other Taxes

I. Sale of Property

425. There is no capital gains tax in New Zealand. Profits on the sale of land and buildings may be regarded as income and thus be taxable if the property is acquired and sold as a business, or speculative proposition rather than as a normal sale of a person's private residence or business. The latter is exempt from tax.

930. Section 51.
931. Section 6.
932. Section 14.
933. Sections 11A, 11AB, 11B.
934. *See,* ss 167–180 and 219–222 of the Accident Compensation Act 2001.

II. Gift and Estate Duty

426. No gift duty is payable in relation to a gift made on or after 1 October 2011, by virtue of section 245 of the Taxation (Tax Administration and Remedial Matters) Act 2011.

427. Estate duty in respect of death occurring on or after 17 December 1992 was abolished in 1993 by the Estate Duty Abolition Act 1993. The relevant part on estate duty in the Estate and Gift Duties Act 1968 was repealed by the Estate Duty Repeal Act 1999.

Chapter 3. Emergency Laws

§1. Wartime Emergency Legislation

428. In times of war, statutes have been introduced to deal with wartime needs. In the past those statutes have given the Governor-General extensive powers to make regulations. Examples were the War Regulations Act 1914, the Emergency Regulations Act 1939 and the Supply Regulations 1947.

In 1918, the War Legislation and Statute Law Amendment Act 1918 was passed. The Act provided that military deserters were to be deprived of their civil rights for ten years from the passing of the Act.[935] Deserters were prohibited from being employed in Crown Service, and could not be members of Parliament or local or public authorities and could not vote at general or local body elections.

§2. General Emergency Legislation

429. Outside of wartime, statutes have often been given extensive emergency powers. The most significant was the Public Safety Conservation Act 1932. The Act which was repealed in 1987 allowed the Governor-General to declare a state of emergency and to promulgate regulations for very broadly defined purposes.[936]

This Act was invoked in 1951 at the time of a waterfront strike. The wide powers of this Act are demonstrated by the Waterfront Strike Emergency Regulations 1951[937] which created a number of offences and gave the police powerful enforcement rights. It was for example an offence to strike, to encourage or incite a strike or to publish material likely to cause a strike.[938]

430. A further Act repealed in 1987, which empowered the making of regulations often to meet emergency or extraordinary situations, was the Economic Stabilisation Act 1948. The purpose of the Act was the promotion of the economic stability of New Zealand.[939] Regulations could be made for a wide variety of reasons relating to economic stability. They were made by the Governor-General as appeared necessary or expedient for promoting economic stability.[940] Over 200 regulations were made pursuant to the Act – many of a controversial nature such as the Wage Freeze Regulations 1982.[941]

---

935. Amending the Expeditionary Forces Act 1915: s. 13.
936. Sections 2 and 3.
937. SR 1951/24.
938. Regulation 4.
939. Section 3.
940. Section 11.
941. SR 1982/141. These put a freeze on wages. In the case of *Combined State Unions v. State Services Co-ordinating Committee* [1982] 1 NZLR 742 the 1982 regulations were declared to be invalid on the grounds that they suspended wage-fixing provisions in an Act. The Economic Stabilisation Amendment Act 1982 gave primacy to the regulations made under that Act over the enabling Act and several other statutes.

431. Now the main statutes dealing with emergency situations are the following:

(a) International Terrorism (Emergency Powers) Act 1987[942] to deal with international terrorist situations.
The Act provides for at least three Ministers of the Crown to authorize the police to exercise emergency powers in terrorist situations. The authority generally expires at the end of the emergency or after seven days whichever is the sooner[943] and may be extended for a limited time by resolution of the House of Representatives[944] or revoked by the House.[945]
Extensive emergency powers are given to the police under the Act to deal with emergencies[946] including, in relation to the area of the emergency, the power to evacuate premises and places, enter (by force if necessary), restrict public access, remove anything which is impeding efforts to deal with the emergency, to requisition property and to destroy property constituting a danger. Members of the armed forces may assist police to deal with an emergency and for that purpose have the same powers as the police.[947]
The Terrorism Suppression Act 2002 makes further provision in New Zealand for the suppression of terrorism and implements New Zealand's obligations under the Bombings Convention, Financing Convention, Anti-terrorism Resolution, Nuclear Material Convention, Plastic Explosives Convention and the Nuclear Terrorism Convention. The Act criminalizes terrorist bombings (section 7), financing of terrorist organizations (section 8) and recruiting and taking part in terrorist movements (sections 12 and 13). The Act also allows for the forfeiture of specified property (section 55).

---

942. An international terrorist emergency is defined in s. 2 as: '"International terrorist emergency" means a situation in which any person is threatening, causing, or attempting to cause – (a) the death of, or serious injury or serious harm to, any person or persons; or (b) the destruction of, or serious damage or serious injury to, – (i) any premises, building, erection, structure, installation, or road; or (ii) any aircraft, hovercraft, ship or ferry or other vessel, train, or vehicle; or (iii) any natural feature which is of such beauty, uniqueness, or scientific, economic, or cultural importance that its preservation from destruction, damage or injury is in the national interest; or(iv) any chattel of any kind which is of significant historical, archaeological, scientific, cultural, literary, or artistic value or importance; or (v) any animal – in order to coerce, deter, or intimidate – (c) the Government of New Zealand, or any agency of the Government of New Zealand; or (d)the Government of any other country, or any agency of the Government of any other country; or (e) any body or group of persons, whether inside or outside New Zealand, – for the purpose of furthering, outside New Zealand, any political aim.'
943. Section 6.
944. Section 7. Pursuant to that section the House of Representatives must be informed that the exercise of emergency powers has been authorized.
945. Section 8.
946. Section 10. Further special powers are given to police to intercept communications: *see,* s. 10(3). Powers are also given to the Prime Minister to prohibit publication or broadcasting of matters relating to a terrorist emergency: *see,* s. 14.
947. Section 12.

The Anti-Money Laundering and Countering Financing of Terrorism Act 2009 also gives supervising powers to monitor, inspect and sanction reporting entities in order to properly enforce compliance with New Zealand's anti-money laundering and countering the finance of terrorism obligations.

(b) There is a provision under the Civil Defence Emergency Management Act 2002 for the declaration of a state of national emergency[948] and for a local emergency.[949] Various powers are given under this statute in such emergencies, such as for evacuation of premises and places, and entry onto premises,[950] for closing of roads and public places[951] for the removal of vehicles[952] and the requisitioning of land or property.[953]

(c) Under the Biosecurity Act 1993, provision is made for the Governor-General by Proclamation to declare a biosecurity emergency. Such an emergency may occur when there is an outbreak or establishment of an organism likely to cause significant environmental or economic loss, or a pest becomes out of control, and it is in the public interest to manage or eradicate the organism or pest.[954] Special emergency powers are given to any Minister of the Crown to deal with the biosecurity emergency, including the requisitioning of craft or premises if that would assist in dealing with the emergency.[955]
The House of Representatives must immediately be informed of a biosecurity emergency, and may extend or revoke a biosecurity emergency, otherwise it expires after four months.[956]
Special regulations may be made by the Governor-General to deal with a biosecurity emergency. Such regulations are automatically revoked after a specified time has elapsed.[957]

(d) The Telecommunications (Interceptions Capability and Security) Act 2013 provides for the lawful interception of telecommunications. The Act requires a network operator to ensure that every public telecommunications network that the operator owns, controls or operates, and every telecommunications service that the operator provides in New Zealand has an interception capacity.[958]

(e) In response to the scale 7.1 Canterbury earthquake on 4 September 2010, the Canterbury Earthquake Response and Recovery Act 2010 was passed under urgency. A second devastating scale 6.3 earthquake followed on 22 February 2011. The Act had a few unusual features. First it allowed secondary legislation to override an Act of Parliament. Section 6 provided that an Order in Council made under the Act could grant exemption from, or modify, or extend any provision of any enactment. Section 7 provided that no Order in Council could be

948. Section 66.
949. Section 68.
950. Sections 86–87.
951. Section 88.
952. Section 89.
953. Section 90.
954. Section 144.
955. Section 145.
956. Sections 146–147.
957. Sections 150 and 151.
958. Section 9.

held invalid because 'it is, or authorizes any act or omission that is, repugnant to or inconsistent with any other Act'. Second, it also allowed an Order in Council made under the Act to have retrospective effect, although not earlier than 4 September 2010. The Act also established a Recovery Commission. The Act was repealed and replaced in April 2011 by the Canterbury Earthquake Recovery Act.

Chapter 4. The Power of the Military

§1. The Military

432. The Act which governs this area is the Defence Act 1990. Key provisions are sections 5 and 11:

> *5.* ***Power to raise armed forces***
> *The Governor-General may from time to time, in the name and on behalf of the Sovereign, continue to raise and maintain armed forces, either in New Zealand or elsewhere, for the following purposes:*
>
> (a) the defence of New Zealand, and of any area for the defence of which New Zealand is responsible under any Act:
> (b) the protection of the interests of New Zealand, whether in New Zealand or elsewhere:
> (c) the contribution of forces under collective security treaties, agreements, or arrangements:
> (d) the contribution of forces to, or for any of the purposes of, the United Nations, or in association with other organizations or States and in accordance with the principles of the Charter of the United Nations:
> (e) the provision of assistance to the civil power either in New Zealand or elsewhere in time of emergency:
> (f) the provision of any public service.

Section 11 identifies the components of the New Zealand Defence Force as the Armed Forces of New Zealand as specified in section 5 and the Civil Staff specified in section 61A.

433. The military forces may be summarized as essentially:

- The New Zealand Naval Forces which is commanded by the Chief of Navy and includes the Royal New Zealand Navy, the Royal New Zealand Naval Reserve, the Royal New Zealand Naval Volunteer Reserve and the Naval Reserves. The role of the Navy incorporates oceanographic research, fisheries protection, search and rescue and sea patrolling.
- The New Zealand Army which is commanded by the Chief of Army. The Army comprises regular, territorial and reserve elements.
- The Royal New Zealand Air Force commanded by the Chief of Air Force. The Air Force comprises regular, territorial and reserve elements. The role of the Air Force is to defend sea and air approaches, to engage in surveillance and air and sea rescue.

434. The defence of New Zealand is the responsibility of the Ministry of Defence and the New Zealand Defence Forces.

The Defence Act 1990 provides for the Secretary of Defence, who is the chief executive of the Ministry of Defence,[959] for the Chief of Defence Force,[960] who is responsible for the New Zealand Defence Force, and for Chiefs of Service, namely Chief of Navy, Chief of Army and Chief of Air Force.[961]

435. The other Act of relevance is the Armed Forces Discipline Act 1971, which provides for the discipline and administration of justice in the armed forces (it broadly covers the Navy, Army and Air Force).[962] The Act specifies offences[963] and details the court martial procedures and constitution and the punishment of offenders.[964]

436. The defence of New Zealand is arguably of low priority since there appear to be no immediate threats to New Zealand from external sources. New Zealand does, however, need to defend itself and protect its sovereignty and, as required, that of the Cook Islands and Niue, and to contribute to internal security, as well as to the general security of the Pacific and to cooperate with other countries to maintain security operations. New Zealand also contributes to the United Nations peace-keeping forces.

437. The military is of value in times of civil defence and terrorist emergencies both in New Zealand and overseas. For example, the Royal New Zealand Air Force and the Navy made relief deliveries to Vanuatu in 2015 after a major cyclone.

It is also useful in times of non-emergency for community assistance. For example, the Navy patrols New Zealand's 200 mile-Exclusive Economic Zone and both the Navy and the Air Force operate search and rescue operations.

438. Additionally, New Zealand has a Security Intelligence Service. The service is governed by the New Zealand Security Intelligence Service Act 1969. The purpose of the service is to obtain and evaluate intelligence relevant to security and to advise ministers on security matters.[965]

The Act provides for the Office of Director of Security, appointed by the Governor-General,[966] who controls the service and provides for the conditions of employees of the Service.[967]

959. Section 24.
960. Section 25.
961. Section 28.
962. Section 6.
963. Part 2, ss 23–77.
964. Sections 78–87A, and Part 9, ss 168–180 and 184–186A (181–183 repealed).
965. Section 4.
966. Section 5.
967. Sections 6 and 8.

§2. POLICE

439. The police are governed by the Policing Act 2008. That Act regulates all matters relating to the police – organization and governance, powers, operations, employments, etc. New Zealand is divided into districts, each controlled by high-ranking officers in the police force. Overall control is vested in the Commissioner of Police who is responsible to the Minister of Police. The Commissioner is appointed by the Governor-General.[968]

The police have the job of maintaining peace and security and detecting and dealing with offences. They also have responsibilities under various other Acts such as the Misuse of Drugs Act 1975 and the Land Transport Act 1998.

The service is largely unarmed. It operates a number of specialist units, such as the Armed Offenders Squad which deals with offenders in possession of weapons, the Anti-terrorist Squad which deals with terrorist emergencies, and a search and rescue operations unit.

440. Complaints against the police may be dealt with by the Independent Police Conduct Authority. The Authority consists of up to five members appointed by the Governor-General on the recommendation of the House of Representatives.[969] The person appointed as the chairperson of the Authority must be a Judge or a retired Judge.[970] The Authority is a Crown entity and the members of the Authority are the board for the purposes of the Crown Entities Act 2004.[971]

The function of the Authority is to hear complaints against the police in respect of alleged misconduct or neglect or concerning policies or practices adopted by the police which affect the complainant in a personal capacity. It may also investigate on its own violation any incidents where a police officer has caused serious bodily harm to a person and review certain police investigations.[972] Complaints are made orally, or in writing.[973] On receipt of a complaint which the Authority decides to proceed with, the Authority must inform the interested parties. The proceedings are held in private[974] and the Authority has the power to request information to be produced and summon people on oath.[975] Witnesses are accorded the same protection as a court witness.[976] After the investigation, the Authority reports its recommendations to the Commissioner of Police[977] and if no action is taken, reports its findings to the Attorney-General and Minister of Police.[978]

968. Section 12.
969. Section 5.
970. Section 5A.
971. Independent Police Conduct Authority Act 1988, s. 4A.
972. Section 12.
973. Section 14.
974. Section 23.
975. Section 24.
976. Section 25.
977. Sections 27 and 28.
978. Section 29.

Chapter 5. The Constitutional Relation between Church and State

441. The New Zealand State is secular; however, there are areas where Church and State matters will inter-relate, such as integrated schools[979] and holidays.[980]

§1. Marriage and the State

442. Pursuant to the Marriage Act 1955, a list of marriage celebrants is held by the Registrar-General.[981] The Act provides that the name of a minister of religion from a body enumerated in the First Schedule, which lists a variety of churches, may be entered on the list; other persons may be approved as marriage celebrants such as those from approved organizations[982] and Justices of the Peace.[983]

Couples intending to marry must give notice to the Registrar of Marriages. Marriages may not be solemnized until a marriage license is issued by the Registrar of Marriages[984] after which the marriage may be solemnized by the marriage celebrant.[985] Marriages may not be solemnized before the Register until three days from the time of notice.[986]

Prior to 2013, a marriage could only be solemnized if it was between a man and a woman. The Civil Union Act, passed in 2004, allows two people, whether they are of different or the same sex, to enter into a civil union. Entering into a civil union involves solemnization of the relationship in a formal ceremony, resulting in registration of the relationship. Legally, it has similar consequences to marriage. As a result of the passing of the Marriage (Definition of Marriage) Amendment Act, a definition of marriage was inserted which reads: 'Marriage means the union of two people, regardless of their sex, sexual orientation, or gender identity'. The current situation is that any couple, regardless of sex, may choose to enter into a marriage or civil union.

Marriage celebrants who are ministers of religion or are nominated to solemnize marriages by an approved organization are not obliged to solemnize a marriage if solemnizing that marriage would contravene the religious beliefs of the religious body of which they are a minister or the religious beliefs or philosophical or humanitarian convictions of the approved organization.

There is a special provision for members of the Quaker religion exempting them from the provisions relating to solemnization of marriages in the presence of marriage celebrants. In that case a certificate signed by the parties and two witnesses to the marriage must be transmitted to the Registrar-General by the Quaker registering officer or one of the parties to the marriage.[987]

---

979. *See*, paragraph 445.
980. Good Friday, Easter Sunday and Christmas.
981. Section 7.
982. Sections 8–10.
983. Section 11.
984. Sections 23, 24 and 30.
985. Section 31.
986. Sections 30 and 33.
987. Section 32.

§2. Taxation of Charities

443. Under the Income Tax Act 2007[988] the term 'charitable purpose' is defined to include purposes for the advancement of religion.

Income obtained by trustees in trust for charitable purposes or by a society established only for charitable purposes is exempt from tax.[989]

Additionally, certain monetary gifts may be allowed as rebates to income tax provided that the gifts are used for charitable purposes which includes religious purposes.[990]

The Charities Act 2005 provides for the registration and monitoring of charities. The Charitable Trusts Act 2005 provides for incorporation of charitable trust boards and management of failed charities.

§3. Private Schools Conditional Integration Act 1975

444. The aim of this Act is to allow private schools to integrate voluntarily and conditionally into the State system while still preserving the special character of the school which is likely to be a religious or philosophical one.

The right to retain the character of the school is provided for in the Act[991] which allows those responsible for determining the special character of the school to continue to supervise the special character of the school and to determine what is necessary to preserve its special character.

988. Section YA 1.
989. Section CW 41.
990. Section LD 1.
991. Section 3.

Selected Bibliography

1. CONSTITUTION

de Smith, S. & R. Brazier. *Constitutional and Administrative Law*. 8th edn. London: Penguin, 1998.
Jennings, I. *The Law and the Constitution*. 5th edn. London: University of London Press Ltd, 1959.
Joseph, P. *Constitutional and Administrative Law in New Zealand*. 4th edn. Wellington: Thomson Brookers, 2014.
Joseph, P. (ed.). *Essays on the Constitution*. Brookers, Wellington, 1995.
McDowell, M. & D. Webb. *The New Zealand Legal System*. 4th edn. Wellington: LexisNexis, 2006.
Palmer, G. *Unbridled Power?: An Interpretation of New Zealand's Constitution and Government*. Wellington: Oxford University Press, 1979.
Palmer, G. *Unbridled Power: An Interpretation of New Zealand's Constitution and Government*. 2nd edn. Auckland: Oxford University Press, 1987.
Palmer, G. *New Zealand's Constitution in Crisis: Reforming our Political System*. Dunedin: John McIndoe, 1992.
Palmer, G. & M. Palmer. *Bridled Power: New Zealand Government under MMP*. 3rd edn. Auckland: Oxford University Press, 1997.
Palmer, G. & M. Palmer. *Bridled Power: New Zealand Government under MMP*. 4th edn. Auckland: Oxford University Press, 2004.
Ringer, J. *An Introduction to New Zealand Government*. Christchurch: Hazard Press, 1991.
Robson, J. *New Zealand: The Development of Its Laws and Constitution*. 2nd edn. London: Stevens, 1967.
Scott, K. *The New Zealand Constitution*. Oxford: Clarendon Press, 1962.
The Laws of New Zealand. Wellington: Butterworths, 1992, loose-leaf volumes.

2. HISTORY

Belich, J. *Paradise Reforged: A History of the New Zealanders from the 1880's to the year 2000*. Auckland: Penguin, 2001.
King, M. *The Penguin History of New Zealand*. Auckland: Penguin, 2003.
Salmond, A. *Two Worlds: First Meetings between Maori and Europeans 1642–1772*. Auckland: Viking, 1991.
Sinclair, K. *History of New Zealand*. Auckland: Penguin, 1991.

3. Freedom of Information

Eagles, I., M. Taggart & G. Liddell. *Freedom of Information in New Zealand*. Auckland: Oxford University Press, 1992.

4. Legislation

Burrows, J. *Statute Law in New Zealand*. 4th edn. Wellington: LexisNexis, 2009.
Carter, Ross, Jason McHerron & Ryan Malone. *Subordinate Legislation in New Zealand* (Wellington: Lexis Nexis, 2013).
Pearce, D. *Delegated Legislation in Australia and New Zealand*. Sydney: Butterworths, 1977.

5. Local Government

Palmer, K. *Local Authorities Law in New Zealand*. 3rd edn. Wellington: Thomson Reuters, 2012.

6. Pacific Territories

Crocombe, R. *The South Pacific*. Suva: University of the South Pacific, 2001.
Douglas, N. *Pacific Islands Yearbook*. 17th edn. Suva: Fiji Times Ltd, 1994.
Gordon, R. *Cook Islands and Niue: A Collection of Legislation Relating to Constitutional Development*. Port Vila, Vanuatu: USP Complex, 1995.
Gordon, R. *Tokelau: A Collection of Documents and References Relating to Constitutional Development*. 2nd edn. Apia: Tokelau Administration, 1995.
Ntumy, M. (ed.). *South Pacific Islands Legal Systems*. Honolulu: University of Hawaii Press, 1993.

7. Parliament and Procedure

McGee, D. *Parliamentary Practice in New Zealand*. 3rd edn. Wellington: Dunmore Publishing, 2005.
Standing Orders of the House of Representatives. Brought into force: 20 February 1996.

8. Politics

Levine, S. *The New Zealand Political System: Politics in a Small Society*. Sydney: George Allen and Unwin, 1979.
Levine, S. & P. Harris. *The New Zealand Politics Source Book*. 3rd edn. Palmerston North: Dunmore Press, 1999.

Miller, Raymond (ed.). *New Zealand Government and Politics*. 5th edn Melbourne: Oxford University Press, 2010.

Mulgan, Richard. *Politics in New Zealand.* 3rd edn Auckland: Auckland University Press, 2003.

9. TREATY OF WAITANGI

Boast, R. *Buying the Land, Selling the Land.* Wellington: Victoria University Press, 2008.

Fenton, Sabine & Paul Moon. 'Survival by Translation'. In *For Better or For Worse: Translation as a Tool for Change in the South Pacific*, edited by Sabine Fenton. Manchester: St Jerome Publishing, 2004.

Kawharu, I. (ed.). *Waitangi: Maori and Pakeha Perspectives on the Treaty of Waitangi.* Auckland: Oxford University Press, 1989.

McHugh, P. *The Maori Magna Carta: New Zealand Law and the Treaty of Waitangi.* Auckland: Oxford University Press, 1991.

Mutu, M. 'The Humpty Dumpty Principle at Work'. In *For Better or For Worse: Translation as a Tool for Change in the South Pacific*. Edited by Sabine Fenton. Manchester: St Jerome Publishing, 2004.

Orange, C. *The Treaty of Waitangi.* Wellington: Allen and Unwin (NZ) Ltd, 1987.

Renwick, W. *Sovereignty and Indigenous Rights: The Treaty of Waitangi in International Contexts.* Wellington: Victoria University Press, 1991.

Palmer, M. *Treaty of Waitangi in New Zealand and Constitution.* Wellington: Victoria University Press, 2008.

Parkinson, P. *The Maori Language and Its Expression in New Zealand Law: Two Essays on the Use of Te Reo Maori in Government and in Parliament.* Wellington: VUWLR, 2001.

Parkinson, P. *Preserved in the Archives of the Colony: The English drafts of the Treaty of Waitangi.* Wellington: New Zealand Association of Comparative Law, 2005.

Selected Bibliography

Index

The numbers here refer to paragraph numbers.

www.ingramcontent.com/pod-product-compliance
Lightning Source LLC
LaVergne TN
LVHW011133300926
849160LV00008B/634